MODERN HUMORIST

presents

Rough Draft

Pop Culture the Way It Almost Was

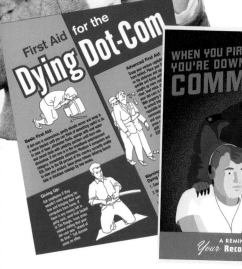

MODERN HUMORIST

presents

Rough Draft

Pop Culture the Way It Almost Was

Edited By
Alexandra Ringe

Designed By
Patrick Broderick

THREE RIVERS PRESS · NEW YORK

"Blowin' in the Wind" lyrics copyright © 1962 by Warner Bros. Inc., copyright renewed 1990 by Special Rider Music. All rights reserved. International copyright secured. Reprinted by permission.

Published by Three Rivers Press, New York, New York.
Member of the Crown Publishing Group.

Random House, Inc. New York, Toronto, London, Sydney, Auckland
www.randomhouse.com

THREE RIVERS PRESS is a registered trademark and the Three Rivers Press colophon is a trademark of Random House, Inc.

Printed in the United States of America

Design by Patrick Broderick/Modern Humorist

Library of Congress Cataloging-in-Publication Data

Modern Humorist presents Rough draft : pop culture the way it almost was / edited by Alexandra Ringe.—1st ed.
    1. Popular culture—United States—History—20th century—Humor.   2. Popular culture—United States—History—20th century—Miscellanea.   3. United States—Civilization—20th century—Humor.   4. United States—Civilization—20th century—Miscellanea.   I. Title: Rough draft.   II. Ringe, Alexandra.   III. Modern Humorist (Firm)

E169.1 .M7147 2001
973.91—dc21   2001023773

ISBN 0-609-80817-6

10 9 8 7 6 5 4 3 2 1

First Edition

MODERN
HUMORIST

presents

Rough Draft

Pop Culture the Way It Almost Was

Written By

John Aboud, Tim Carvell, Michael Colton, Laura Gilbert,
Josh Greenman, Kevin Guilfoile, Francis Heaney, Krister M. Johnson,
Martha Keavney, Michael Francis Martone, Daniel Radosh, Alexandra Ringe,
Beth Sherman, Thomas Talbot, Noam Weinstein, Steve Zimet

Additional Material By

Patrick Broderick, Daniel Chun, Daniel J. Goor, Charlie Grandy,
Fred Graver, David King, Lauren Kirchner, Gersh Kuntzman, Seth Mnookin,
Nick Nadel, Eben Russell, Jeremy Simon, Michael Sloan,
Geoffrey Stevens, Nicholas A. Stoller, John Warner

Additional Art By

Ivan Brunetti, Marc Crisafulli, Zach Fried, Danny Hellman, John R. Holmes,
Vance Lehmkuhl, Jason Little, Dyna Moe, R. Sikoryak, William Wu

Special Thanks To

Kate Barker, Rebecca Clement, TJ Connelly, Pete Fornatale, Louis Giliberti,
Roy Hall, Eric Kissack, Avi Muchnick, Kim Witherspoon

Concept inspired by "First Drafts" material written by
Daniel J. Goor and Charlie Grandy

Modern Humorist Founders

John Aboud and Michael Colton

PHOTO CREDITS:

ILLUSTRATION CREDITS:

About the Author

Modern Humorist, an entertainment company based in Brooklyn, produces an award-winning daily comedy magazine at ModernHumorist.com. Modern Humorist also creates material for *Time*, *Fortune*, *TV Guide*, *Yahoo! Internet Life*, VH1.com, and National Public Radio. Its first book was *My First Presidentiary: A Scrapbook by George W. Bush*, written by contributing editors Kevin Guilfoile and John Warner. Its first movie was *Splendor in the Grass*.

To give your feedback about this book, or to find out more about Modern Humorist, send a message to roughdraft@ modernhumorist.com. Additional information is available at ModernHumorist.com/RoughDraft.

Contents

> ## *"Nobody gets it right the first time, not even Elvis."*
>
> **— Elvis Presley**

The planners of Woodstock got it wrong the first time. No one wanted to see "Three Days of Peace, Love, and Monster Trucks." Until his producer convinced him otherwise, Mister Rogers wanted to start every show in a Dallas Cowboys half-shirt. Likewise, Paramount was going to release *Forrest Gump* as *American Retard*. Oprah thought a Beer Club would be more popular than a Book Club.

Fortunately, none of these ideas saw the light of day. But there are many more like them: Behind every box-office smash, bestselling book, hit television show, or popular putty-based toy lies a Rough Draft. It is the creator's original vision in its purest form—before "market research," before "focus groups," before "constructive criticism."

For the first time ever, these forgotten blueprints of the creative process have been gathered into a single volume containing 128 pages *and* an index. From the Three Stooges to Jerry Springer, from Barbie to Britney, this book presents 20th-century popular culture in its birthday suit. Librarians and custodians around the country have helped us rescue nearly 500 Rough Drafts from the national wastebasket.

We hope you enjoy Modern Humorist's *Rough Draft*, but we also hope you absorb the lessons within. As Judy Garland once noted, "You can learn a lot from completely fabricated 'historical' documents intended as satirical jabs at American pop culture. Now get your feet off my Adidas, bitch."

*"All right, Mr. DeMille.
I'm ready for my money shot."*

— Norma Desmond in *Sunset Boulevard* (1950)

Chapter One
1900-1959

THE *Miss America* PAGEANT

OFFICIAL PROGRAM ▪ ATLANTIC CITY, NEW JERSEY

◀ At the first Miss America Pageant (1921), the crown went to the young woman whose figure bore the closest resemblance to the forty-eight states.

◀ This rib-eye prototype of the Lego (1932) began to smell and attract flies shortly after its invention.

◀ Thong underwear, both the style shown here and an all-fabric version, was first introduced at the 1939 World's Fair.

Walt Disney ▶ discovered and removed this "Steamboat Willie" sequence minutes before the cartoon's 1928 premiere. He then fired the animator who was responsible in front of all his friends.

From *Casablanca* (1942)

RICK BLAINE
Here's lookin' at your ass, kid.

Named for "sweet ▶ milk chocolate," S&M's became M&M's (1941) due to Mars Confections' fears of alienating customers who prefer dark chocolate.

OREO SANDWICHES

Oh! Oh!

It's Oreo!

Rich White Creme, Crunchy Chocolate-Flavored Center

When the Oreo debuted in 1912, it featured two icing layers and one cookie.

as
rite
aps
hould
l-life

Mr. Mashed Potato Head (1949) was followed by Mr. Scalloped Potato Head (1951).

In an early draft written after Judy Garland signed on,
The Wizard of Oz (1939) does not have a happy ending.

INT. FARMHOUSE

Dorothy lying on bed, mumbling. Auntie Em and Uncle Henry
watch, worried. Dorothy opens her eyes, looks around
room.

                    DOROTHY
    -- no place like home -- there's no place
    like home -- no place --

                    AUNTIE EM
    Dorothy. Dorothy, dear, wake up...It's Aunt
    Em, darling.

                    DOROTHY
    Oh, Auntie Em, it's you! But this can't be
    home, can it? Everything's so black and so
    white --

Hunk, Hickory and Zeke enter, kneel beside
bed.

                    UNCLE HENRY
    She got quite a bump on the head. We kinda
    thought there for a minute she was going to
    leave us.

                    DOROTHY
    But I _did_ leave you, Uncle Henry. I went
    over the rainbow to a place filled with
    gorgeous colors and charming, drunken
    midgets who worshipped me. And I had these
    fabulous red shoes.

                    AUNTIE EM
    There, there, lie quiet now. You just had a
    bad dream.

                    DOROTHY
    But it wasn't a dream -- it was a place --
    a beautiful and exciting place.

                    HUNK
    Cheer up, Dorothy -- don't you remember
    your old pal, Hunk?

                    ZEKE
    You couldn't forget my face, could you?

                    DOROTHY
    No -- no you -- and you -- and you -- were
    there with me, not as homely farmhands but
    as delightful personifications of human
    foibles who could dance and sing.

                    AUNTIE EM
    Oh, we dream lots of silly things when we --

                    DOROTHY
    Don't patronize me. Just because I'm
    wearing pigtails and my breasts are bound
    and I'm on uppers doesn't mean you can
    treat me like a child.

                    UNCLE HENRY
    Dorothy, sweetheart, maybe you should try
    to rest.

                    DOROTHY
    (eyes closed, muttering bitterly) All I
    kept saying to everybody was, "There's no
    place like home. Forget Oz, forget all the
    fun and the costumes and the dance numbers
    -- I really want to go to that depression-
    era farm back in Kansas." Christ! What a
    disappointment I must be to gay men
    everywhere!

FADE OUT

From *Citizen Kane* (1941)

                    BERNSTEIN
    She was carrying a white parasol. I
    only saw her for one second. She didn't
    see me at all, but I'll bet a month
    hasn't gone by since that I haven't
    masturbated while thinking of that girl.

HOOF-O

GELATIN.

LEMON FLAVOR.

Before coming
up with the
name Jell-O,
the Genesee
Pure Food
Company
considered the
packaging
shown here,
hoping to hide
the fact that
gelatin is
made of hide
trimmings.

The 101 Stooges, partial group portrait, 1922. Front row: Spats Clark, Popeye Sneed, Fanny Shoemaker, Red Bryant. Second row: Blossom Smithers, Tiger Lily McCoy, Happy Eva Turnbull, Gus the Bus Miller. Third row: Curly Howard, Larry Fine, Annie T. Skidoo, Trixie Trent, Moe Howard, Honey Gold, Eva LaTour, Fingers Edwards. Fourth row: Ada Gallagher, Murray Kemp, Easy Lew Weber, Whistling Pete Russell, Bert Bayer, Bunny O'Leary, Charlie Boggs, Big Lucy Cotton, Marty McGinty, Dickie Napier, Harlan Meeker, Whiskey Porter.

In 1923 the 101 Stooges were winnowed to three: Red Bryant, Larry Fine, and Big Lucy Cotton. Bryant and Cotton were hemophiliacs, so in their early vaudeville skits the Stooges were very careful to make sure no one got hurt. Soon Bryant and Cotton were replaced by Moe and Shemp Howard, who were not hemophiliacs but did bruise easily.

From *Casablanca* (1942)

```
              RICK BLAINE
Louis, I think this is the beginning of
a healthy sexual relationship.
```

In a 1937 meeting with National Periodical Publications, Jerry Siegel and Joe Shuster proposed a comic about Superman, a gossip columnist for a New York City tabloid who uses his special powers to scoop the competition.

◀ "Who was that mud-masked man? He's the crimefighter with spotless pores!" This was the tag line for the Lone Ranger, who first appeared in 1940s magazine ads for Nite Creme.

When it was first introduced on the market, the color television set was comprised of a large mirror, costumes, props, and scripts for *The Milton Berle Show*.

NOTHING ELSE IS
Silly GRouT
THE REAL SOLID LIQUID

◀ Inventor James Wright was sent back to the drawing board after this product failed to draw children to hardware stores.

Decorative white ▶ frosting was added to Hostess chocolate cupcakes in 1950. Later, with the opening of the company's first factory, automation turned the designs into illegible squiggles.

THE CATCHER IN THE RYE
By J.D. Salinger

CHAPTER ONE

If you really want to hear about it, the first thing you'll probably want to know is where you can buy ammunition, and find a gun store that doesn't do background checks, and all that kind of crap, but I don't feel like going into it, if you want to know the truth. In the first place, that stuff bores me, and in the second place, do a little work yourself, for crying out loud. There's nothing I hate worse than a phony who wants you to do all their work for them. I just want to tell you about this madman stuff that happened to me last Christmas, because somehow I think you'll relate. I mean that's all I told D.B. about, and he's my <u>brother</u> and all. He used to be in this terrific band called The Secret Bananafish, in case you never heard of him. They used to play in the cellar of a tiny little bar downtown. They <u>killed</u> me. Now he's on the Upper West Side, making loads of dough and living in a hotel with his phony Japanese artist wife. If there's one thing I hate, it's people who are rich and married to <u>conceptual artists.</u> Don't even mention it to me.

The opening of Salinger's oddly prescient rough draft.

In the late 1890s, the economic theory of low supply creating high demand inspired this licorice treat. Each box contained three, sometimes four, pieces of candy.

Reddi Wip original formula contained no cream. Sales were very good.

The first Eames chair (1945), nicknamed "Sittin' Pretty."

The Slinky started out as the Stiffy, a solid cylinder of metal, and was distributed to toy stores in 1945. At left, the original radio jingle.

```
STIFFY SPOT
(To be sung by young boy)

It rolls down stairs,
Not well, but who cares,
And makes a clunkity sound.
A tube! A tube!
Why, only a boob
Would not want to buy a Stiffy.
It's Stiffy, it's Stiffy,
Just slightly less fun than a ball.
It's Stiffy, it's Stiffy--
It's better than no toy at all.
It's better than no toy at all.


3/14/44
```

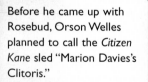

Before he came up with Rosebud, Orson Welles planned to call the Citizen Kane sled "Marion Davies's Clitoris."

In 1944, after three years of publishing Archie Comics, creator John L. Goldwater added the love triangle between his protagonist, Betty, and Veronica. In the galley proofs of the first issue, Betty and Veronica shared more than a crush on a redheaded boy.

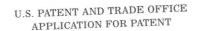

U.S. PATENT AND TRADE OFFICE APPLICATION FOR PATENT

NAME OF INVENTION: PEZ DISPENSER

ABSTRACT:

The "PEZ Dispenser" (fig. 1) is an item that delivers PEZ candy to the consumer in a unique and entertaining manner.

The PEZ candy is loaded into the "candy chamber" (fig. 2) of the "dispenser." Each "candy chamber" holds six pieces of PEZ candy.

Once loaded, the consumer will aim the "dispenser" (fig. 3) towards his/her mouth and then pull a "trigger device" (fig. 4) to launch the candy.

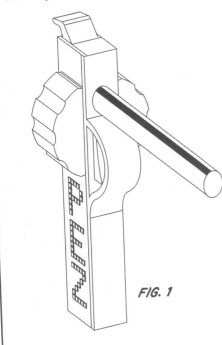

FIG. 1

FIG. 2

FIG. 3

FIG. 4

Work-Doh—"industrial strength clay for all your office clay needs"— was stocked in offices everywhere in the early 1950s, but the Doh fell out of favor by 1955 when the clay-boss-voodoo trend took hold.

The first design for the PEZ dispenser (1948) was rejected on legal grounds.

Great idea but brings up some issues of liability. We'd prefer it if the candy didn't shoot out of the dispenser at 409 mph. Also, the gun shape is going to be a bear to clear. Let's meet and find some middle ground.

           —BILL

SUPER HIGH-TECH GIZMOS 23/7/52

(Must include in Casino Royale)

- combination chef knife/fillet knife

- "wrap-around" sunglasses

- whitening toothpaste disguised as yellowing toothpaste

- American Express card with unlimited credit

- machine capable of transliterating Hebrew prayers into English

- self-hardening penis with ability to shoot semen

- ballpoint pen disguised as fountain pen

- adjustable baseball cap

- laminated license to kill

◀ Ian Fleming based this list on his experiences as a British Naval Intelligence officer.

From *To Have and Have Not* (1944)

SLIM
You know how to whistle, don't you, Steve? You just utter a shrill, clear sound by drawing air through your puckered lips.

Radio stations ▶ shortened the title of this 1955 hit without Haley's permission.

BILL HALEY And His COMETS

RECORD NO. 1

SIDE NO. 1

45 RPM

Rock Until Roughly 9:30, At Which Point The Band Breaks For Gunsmoke: Then, Prerecorded Jazz Around The Clock

Designs considered for Dr Pepper's relaunch in cans (1954).

The ASPCA was horrified by Davy Crockett's shar-pei skin cap. Threatened with bad publicity, Disney changed it to coonskin before the show debuted in 1954.

▶ Users of this early version of the remote control complained that it took as long as ten minutes to switch from one of the three television channels to another.

In the first draft ▶ of Kay Thompson's *Eloise* (1955), the protagonist has the same profile as the subsequently published Eloise. She lives in the Plaza, owns a dog and a turtle, steals things from hotel guests, hides bottle caps in her kneesocks and has a nanny. The only difference? She is fifty-five years old.

Getting bored is not allowed
Sometimes I comb my hair with a fork

Sometimes I wear my arm in a sling

Sometimes I put a rubber band on the end of my nose

Toe shoes make very good ears
Sometimes I wear them to lunch

On the set of *Rebel Without a Cause* (1955), it was Sal Mineo who encouraged James Dean to try cigarettes in lieu of his customary pipe. ▶

◀ ADJUSTABLE ▶

Barbara

BARBARA DOLL INCLUDES:
- Sensible SHOES
- Prescription EYEGLASSES
- Change of CLOTHES

NOTHING MORE TO BUY!

◀ "Barbara," a doll based on the inventor's fifth grade teacher, rolled off the assembly line in 1958.

➡ Every single recipient of the first Publishers Clearing House Sweepstakes mailing threw out the letter unopened.

PUBLISHERS CLEARING HOUSE SWEEPSTAKES

YOU MAY HAVE ALREADY WON

A MAGAZINE SUBSCRIPTION!

James Mercer
14 Caravella Drive Apt 4
San Jose, CA 95117

This scene was cut from ▶ *The Seven-Year Itch* (1955) due to a contract dispute involving Larry "Midget" Flanagan.

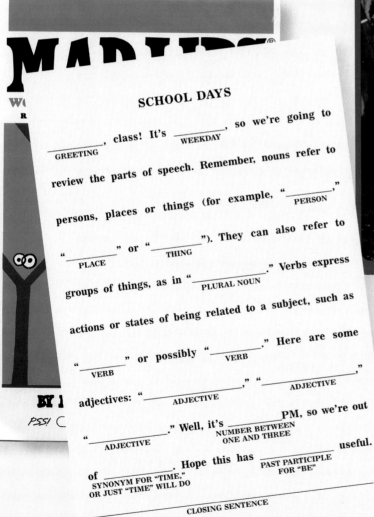

SCHOOL DAYS

_____, class! It's _____, so we're going to
GREETING   WEEKDAY

review the parts of speech. Remember, nouns refer to

persons, places or things (for example, "_____,"
                                          PERSON

"_____" or "_____"). They can also refer to
   PLACE   THING

groups of things, as in "_____." Verbs express
                          PLURAL NOUN

actions or states of being related to a subject, such as

"_____" or possibly "_____." Here are some
   VERB   VERB

adjectives: "_____," "_____,"
              ADJECTIVE   ADJECTIVE

"_____." Well, it's _____PM, so we're out
   ADJECTIVE   NUMBER BETWEEN
                          ONE AND THREE

of _____. Hope this has _____ useful.
   SYNONYM FOR "TIME,"   PAST PARTICIPLE
   OR JUST "TIME" WILL DO   FOR "BE"

_____.
              CLOSING SENTENCE

◀ Initially Mad Libs (1958) were a bit less whimsical.

Before introducing the solid-body electric guitar in 1951, Leo Fender tried to interest musicians in his prototype solid-body electric cello. Although the 700-pound hand-carved hardwood instrument was visually appealing, its tendency to distort and feed back kept it from catching on.

the Bat Who Shat
the Yak in Shellac
the Moose in the Noose
the Mole Who Chews Skoal
the Fox Who Sucks Cocks
The Whale Reading Braille
the Rhino that's a Wino
the Seal that's Gonorrheal
the Wolverine in the Latrine
the Chinchilla in the Flotilla
the Salmon that Cheats at Backgammon
the Llama in the Police Drama
the Koala Who Rules Valhalla
the Manatee Who Uses Profanity
the Cow Who Acts All Holier than thou
the Capybara Who likes Carbonara
the Moray Eel in the Stolen Automobile
the Ring-Tailed Lemur Shunned for being a Blasphemer
the Bison Whose Skin Condition Requires Erythromycin
the three-toed Sloth who writes Under the pseudonym
Phillip Roth
the Panda Handing Out Anti-American Propaganda
the Shark that Suddenly Evolved and Gained the Ability
to Breathe Air, in Accordance with the theories of Lamarck

These drawings, for a proposed series targeted at older readers, were found among the effects of Theodor Geisel (Dr. Seuss), creator of *The Cat in the Hat* (1957).

The GIRAFFe in the CARAFe

THE HORSE going through a PAINFUL DIVORCE

The WOMBAT who was KILLED in COMBAT

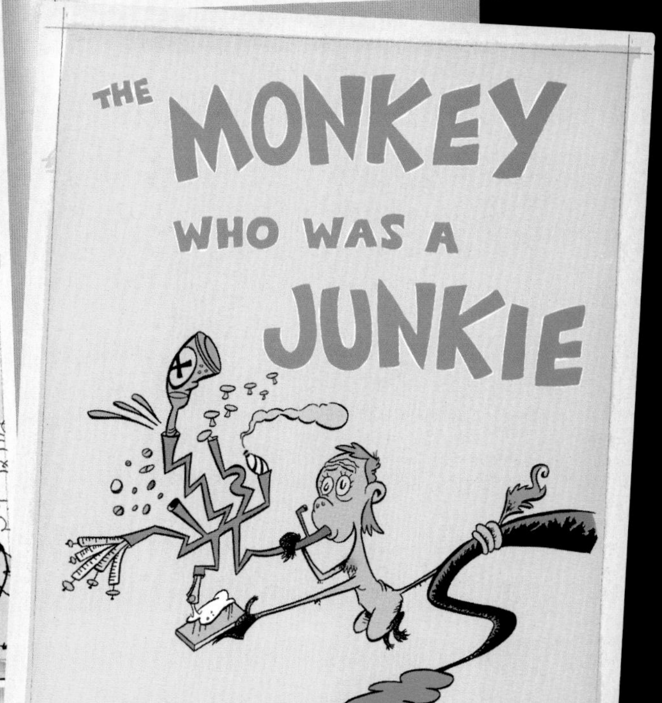

THE MONKEY WHO WAS A JUNKIE

These lyrics for the *Mickey Mouse Club* signoff song frightened Walt Disney's secretary so badly that she resigned on the spot.

FROM THE DESK OF (Walt Disney)

SANDY—
PLEASE TYPE THIS UP: —WALT

THE GOOD-BYE SONG

M-I-C ... SEE YOU IN HEAVEN WHEN OUR GREAT LEADER MICKEY GIVES US THE SIGNAL TO TAKE OUR OWN LIVES!

K-E-Y ... WHY? BECAUSE WE LOVE MICKEY AND HAVE DEDICATED OUR LIVES TO SERVING HIM!

M-O-U-S-E!

The Pack Rats began saving newspapers, bottles, cans, and twine in 1957. Shown here are the collections with which they traveled. The Rats generally left their auto parts and other large keepsakes at home.

126 ELVIS FANS CAN'T BE WRONG

ELVIS' FIRST RECORD - Volume 1

A FOOL SUCH AS I
I NEED YOUR LOVE TONIGHT
WEAR MY RING AROUND YOUR NECK
DONCHA' THINK IT'S TIME
I BEG OF YOU
A BIG HUNK O' LOVE
DON'T
MY WISH CAME TRUE
ONE NIGHT
I GOT STUNG

While still performing at local diners, Elvis Presley sold copies of his first album from the back of his father's pickup truck.

"Turn over, hit snooze button, wake up at 10."

— Timothy Leary before he learned how
to "turn on, tune in, drop out"

Chapter Two
1960-1969

When cartoonist Bil Keane came
up with the idea of a family of circus
freaks, he knew he was sitting on a
gold mine. Mommy would be the
Fat Lady, Daddy would have lobster
claws, Billy would be the Frog Boy,
PJ would have a tail, Dolly would
be covered in fur, and Jeffy would
be a pinhead. Keane's friends loved
the idea, except the part about the
circus and the freakish traits.

THE CIRCUS FAMILY   by Bil Keane

"Thelma, have you seen my shaving cream?"

THE CIRCUS FAMILY   by Bil Keane

"Who let the trained bears in the house?!?"

THE CIRCUS FAMILY   by Bil Keane

"No, PJ, just because you have a tail,
it doesn't mean you're a fairy."

In 1963 *Sports Illustrated* ▶ attempted to attract a broader demographic by covering "the issues that women really care about, like staying warm." When the cover shown here bombed on the newsstands, *SI* switched to swimsuits, citing "another issue that women really care about: giving their husbands a reason to masturbate after the football season ends."

Sports Illustrat

DECEMBER 7, 1963

THE BARE MAX
Layering in L

FIRST ANN
SNOWSUIT

Miss Andrews--

Remember: midnight tomorrow, studio G.
Thank you so much for doing this.
Yours with a spoonful of sugar-- *RMS*

Um diddle diddle diddle um diddle ay
Um diddle diddle diddle um diddle ay
Supercalifuckyoudisneypaymemybackwages!

My lawyer tried to warn me when
I went to work for Walt
I'd get no fees for royalties,
It's all that asshole's fault
So though I signed a contract I
Won't write another note
But now he says he'll sue me so
Here is the song I wrote:

Oh, supercalifuckyoudisneypaymemybackwages!
Aren't you happy, here's your song I
Ground out seven pages
Don't you treat me like a serf, it's
Not the Middle Ages
Supercalifuckyoudisneypaymemybackwages!

◀ Although some disgruntled actors and writers have successfully planted subversive messages in children's classics, irregularities in the first recording of *Mary Poppins*'s "Supercalifragilisticexpialidocious" (1964) were caught in time to be overdubbed in post-production.

In th
Dr. N
Bonc
was
"In a
And

The o
F
gov
beca
desig

fox f
thou
thre
slow
coa
extr
sligh
nati
bag,
even
eight
but ei
altho
runw
eight
pink
open-
gloss
pock
smas
vivid
beau
the V
wom
beau
unde

PARIS IS "ABUZZ" *about the newest hair style to hit the runways this spring. Called the "Beehive," the coif requires 1,000 live bees. Though painstaking to create, the elegant 'do provides the wearer with both sophistication and raw honey.*

aris in the springtime is indeed lovely, and so

◀ The original beehive was created by female French entomologists who wanted to look sexy yet professional on the job.

T.G.I. Friday's, which opened its first restaurant in 1965, started out as Thank Yahweh It's Friday's.

Due to a near-fatal ▶ accident involving a game of chicken and a girl named Pam, Ralph Nader's first book was postponed and retitled *Unsafe at Any Speed* (1965).

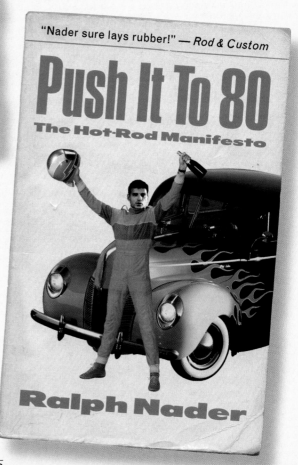

"Nader sure lays rubber!" — *Rod & Custom*

Push It To 80
The Hot-Rod Manifesto

Ralph Nader

Early in the development phase, Lucky Charms cereal (1964) was divided proportionally to reflect Irish politics and geography. The gold crown marshmallows went into the two-ounce Protestant box, while the twelve-ounce Catholic box contained five kinds of marshmallows: blue crosses, yellow potatoes, green shamrocks and brown pints of Guinness.

From *Psycho* (1960)

```
          NORMAN
Mother, my mother -- uh, what
is the phrase? -- she isn't
qu-quite herself today. She's dead.
I killed her. Check-out is at 11.
```

◀ Before settling for the miniskirt, fashion designers tried miniaturizing a number of other items, including pants, shoes, glasses, and sweaters (shown here).

➤ In 1962 the Beatles included John Lennon, Paul McCartney, George Harrison, and a rotating group of accompanists. Their music was innovative, but scheduling was nearly impossible, forcing the three primary members to make cuts. Shown here are Lennon's notes from a long, drunken night of deliberations.

MICHAEL JAGGER – vocals – freakish-looking
B. BACHARACH – keyboards – wants to take the band in a different direction
JUDI DENCH – oboe – open to shagging but can't carry a tune
N. DIAMOND – vocals – always singing over my solos
HENRY MANCINI – eh
JIMI HENDRIX – guitar – no respect for the equipment
DESI ARNAZ – bandleader – too much Babalu, not enough Louie, Louie
BRIAN WILSON – guitar, theremin – snobbish
BOB DYLAN – vocals – absolutely <u>brilliant</u> but the whining...
JIM HENSON – puppetry – Paul's recruit – THE BAND DOESN'T
          NEED ANY BLOODY PUPPETS
PAULINE KAEL – called my songs "jejune"
IAN McKELLEN – bass – always trying to get Paul tipsy
PETER TORK
MIKE NESMITH   ⎫ swell blokes but haven't
MICKY DOLENZ   ⎬ contributed much musically
DAVY JONES   ⎭
J.D. SALINGER – xylophone – silent but deadly
GEORGE LAZENBY – leaving anyway for "bigger things"
ALEX TREBEK – trombone – Canadian
JOHN GIELGUD – flute – lends band a touch of class,
          precisely what we don't want
MARGARET THATCHER – tambourine – looks too much like Benny Hill
IKE TURNER – bass – slapped George
PETER NOONE – guitar – wants to change the band's name
          to Herman's Hermits

RALPH NADER – sousaphone – no
RAY MANZAREK – keyboards – creepy
MORLEY SAFER – drums – too much of a wild man
(RINGO STARR) – adequate drummer, has incriminating
          photos of me & Brian – HE STAYS

PETE BEST – wanker
STU SUTCLIFFE – wanker

This series became ▶ *Richie Rich* (1960) in response to a sharp rise in income among comic readers (due to innovations in paper routes and drug pushing).

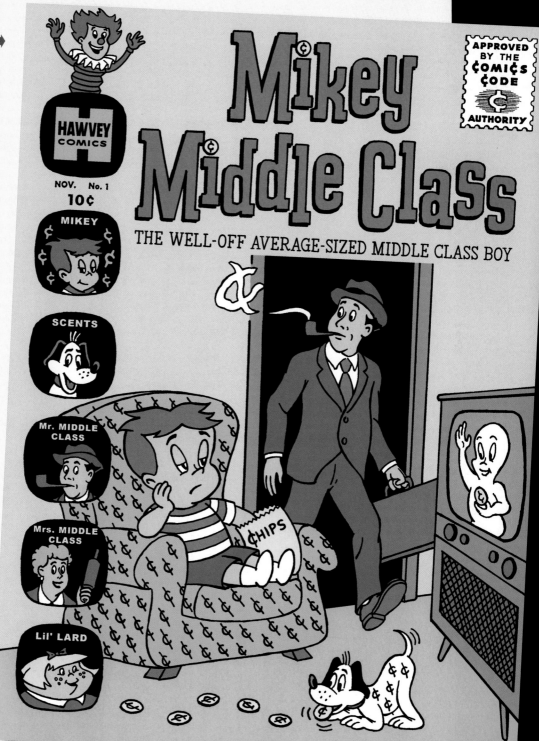

Janet Leigh refused to enact Alfred Hitchcock's original vision for the shower scene in *Psycho* (1960) for fear of offending her fan base, which at the time was comprised mainly of plumbers.

MARION STEPS INTO SHOWER

TURNS ON WATER

SHOWER HEADS ARE SCARY!

SENSUOUS LATHERING

HOT WATER FAUCET IS LOOSE — AND MARION DOESN'T REALIZE IT!

OH NO!

SHOWER HEAD AGAIN! SCARY!

MARION SCREAMS AND JUMPS — SHOCK OF COLD WATER MUST BE PALPABLE!

NOTE TO SET DESIGNER — NO RUBBER FLOWER STICKERS ON BOTTOM OF TUB.

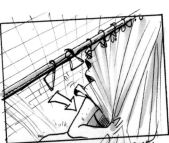

THE SHAMPOO MUST BE "NO MORE TEARS" — THE IRONY WILL BE OH SO DELICIOUS.

NOTE — BUY CHEAP SHOWER CURTAIN — DON'T WASTE MONEY ON SOMETHING WE'RE JUST GOING TO RUIN

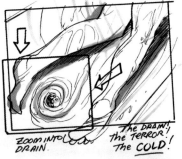

ZOOM INTO DRAIN.

THE DRAIN! THE TERROR! THE COLD!

In 1960, the Ohio Art Company developed the Etch-A-Sketch, a sophisticated desktop mechanism with a handheld pointing device. Its purpose was to enable children to draw without pencil or paper. Unfortunately, the price per unit—$87,000 plus tax—was prohibitive, so the company removed the box behind the screen, the box under the screen, and the "mouse."

The plot of *Easy Rider* (1969) originally included a plot.

Muhammad Ali delighted the media with his lyrical braggadocio, exemplified by "Float like a butterfly, sting like a bee" (1964). But early in his career, the young Cassius Clay was more tentative and lacked an adequate rhyming dictionary.

COLUMBIA AUDITORIUM · LOUISVILLE, KY

I KNOW A BOXER NAMED TOMMY HUNSAKER.
IF HE THINKS HE'LL BEAT ME,
HE SURE IS ONE SUCKER.
PLEASE DON'T TELL HIM I SAID THAT.

Blowin' in the Wind

How many roads must a man walk down before
you call him a man? Three hundred.
Yes and how many seas must a white dove sail
before she sleeps in the sand? Seventy.
Yes and how many times must the cannon balls fly
before they've forever banned? Eight thousand & six.

chorus {
The answers my friend are three hundred, seventy,
and eight thousand and six.
The answers are three hundred, seventy, and
eight thousand and six.

How many times must a man look up before he can
see the sky? Fourteen.
Yes and how many ears must one man have before
he can hear people cry? One.
Correct and how many deaths will it take 'till he knows
that too many people have died? Three dozen.

chorus {
The answers my friend are fourteen, one and 3 dozen.
The answers add up to fifty·one.

How many years can a mountain exist before it is
washed to the sea? Lots.
Yes and how many years can some people exist
before they're allowed to be free? Depends.
Good and how many times can a man turn his
head, pretending he just doesn't see? Infinity.

The answers my friend are lots, depends and infinity.
The answers are lots, depends and infinity.

$$\begin{array}{r} 22 \\ 5239 \\ 1781 \\ 986 \\ \hline 8006 \end{array}$$

$$197\overline{)2758}\;\;14$$

$x^2 + \log X$

Seizing on young boys' interest in belching and defecating, Hasbro experimented with Gastro-Intestinal Joe, a soldier in the war against acid indigestion.

G-I JOE

From _Dr. No_ (1962)

```
            BOND
Bond.  James Bond.  James Susan Bond.
```

In 1960 Betty Friedan invented a feminine hygiene product that promised to win "men, friends, and fun" by masking embarrassing odors. After disappointing sales, Friedan grew extremely bitter toward the male-dominated marketplace and channeled her outrage into a groundbreaking book on women's rights.

Fresh New Scent!

The
Feminine Mystique
Disposable Douche

B. Friedan
BEAUTY, INC.

Alcohol Free · Floral Fragrance

RODGERS AND HAMMERSTEIN'S

THE SMELL OF ODOR

Starring J
AND

Directed by
ROBERT WISE

RODGERS AND HAMMERSTEIN'S

THE FEEL OF TOUCH

Starr
A

Directed by
ROBERT WIS

RODGERS AND HAMMERSTEIN'S

THE TASTE OF FOOD

Starring JULIE
ANDREWS   and   CHRISTOPHER
PLUMMER

Directed by
ROBERT WISE | Music by
RICHAR D ROGERS | Lyrics by
OSCAR HAMMERSTEIN II

The BEATLES

000017

Before John Lennon rejected the idea as "a bit too fruity, even for us," the Beatles' *White Album* (1967) was meant to be colored using a specially mixed puce ink (Pantone 700C).

To differentiate the stage production of *The Sound of Music* from his big-screen version (1965), director Robert Wise tried some new titles. In the end, his only change was making the Nazi cute.

THE GAME THAT IS LIKELY TO STRETCH YOUR LOWER CALVES

MB MILTON BRADLEY

FOR AGES 6 and Up

MILTON BRADLEY COMPANY SPRINGFIELD MASSACHUSETTS

LEFT FOOT · RIGHT HAND · LEFT HAND · RIGHT FOOT

Twister THE GAME THAT MAKES KNEELING FUN

▲ Concerned about being held liable for injuries, Milton Bradley executives initially insisted on a much simpler version of Twister (1966) that had only two dots.

MAKE LOVE NOT FARTS

◀ This slogan was first coined by Missy Banks, a sixth grader and amateur button-maker in La Jolla, California. Marxist philosopher Herbert Marcuse met Missy at a bus stop on his way to a talk on student activism and felt that with a new ending—"not war"—her message would be the perfect refrain for his lecture.

Neil Simon considered and rejected many pairings for his play *The Odd Couple* (1965) before settling on, in his words, "Chief Big Slob and the Nelly Pantywaist."

One is tall, one is short
One is allergic to cats, one is a strange cat/human hybrid
One has multiple personalities, one has NO personality
One is John F. Kennedy, one is Richard Nixon
One is a serial killer, one is a rebel cop who follows his own rules
One is male, one is female
One is American, one comes from a fictional foreign country
    with a funny accent
One is a child raised by wolves, one is a wolf raised by
            children
One is a pyromaniac, one likes to pee on things
One writes fan letters to Audrey Hepburn, one thinks
    he is Audrey Hepburn
One is an irresistible force, one is an immovable object
One wants to commit genocide, one has bad penmanship
One is a Druid, one is a Zoroastrian
One is obsessively neat, one keeps hitting the other one
    in the head with a cricket bat
One is a barber, one glues hair on people
One is a pastry chef, one is a talking bee
One is deaf, one just shouts and shouts and shouts
One is gay, one is bi-curious
One is sloppy, one is really sloppy
One is happy-go-lucky, one is dead

"What an Odd Couple!"
(Too long?)

Until PBS objected, Mister Rogers started his television show by removing his blazer to reveal this half-shirt. He argued futilely that children would more readily identify with a man who loves his team than a man who wears zip-up cardigans.

In the second version of *Family Circus* (see p. 34), Ida Know and Not Me, the ghosts that get blamed for all sorts of mishaps, were named Fuckih Fino and Yoocan Blowme.

This
is
Benjamin

He's
a little
worried
about
his
future

THE GRAD

STARRING **JOE BANCROFT** AND **DUSTIN HOFFMAN · K**

POCKET EDITIONS $ .95

Everything you always wanted to know about sex*

* BUT WERE STILL CONFUSED ABOUT, EVEN AFTER FINDING YOUR FATHER'S PORN STASH AT THE BOTTOM OF HIS SOCK DRAWER

The Graduate (1967) originally focused on a recent college grad's ambiguous friendship with a local firefighter. Joe Bancroft, who was cast as the fireman, came down with pneumonia just before shooting began, but he managed to put director Mike Nichols in touch with his stepsister Anne, also an actor.

Although David Reuben changed his book's subtitle to "but were afraid to ask" and expanded its content accordingly, he neglected to explain, as one reviewer put it, "why people's faces look so damn funny when they're coming."

PROPERTY OF
Desilu.
PRODUCTION DEPARTMENT

For *Star Trek*'s 1966 debut, Desilu's wardrobe consultants knew they needed something that would quickly identify Mr. Spock as non-human. Their first attempt prevented Leonard Nimoy from resting comfortably during breaks, so the pointy prostheses were moved to his ears.

Before its publication in 1969, the bible of the self-help movement went through several titles, including the one shown here and *I'm OK, You're OK for a One Night Stand*.

Thomas A. Harris, M.D.

I'M OK, FUCK YOU

A PRACTICAL GUIDE TO TRANSACTIONAL ANALYSIS

are you meant to be married?

A COSMO QUIZ
BY
ERNEST DICHTER, PH.D.

For each question, circle the answer that you think will give you the most desirable rating at the end of the quiz.

1. You are a:
a. Size 2.
b. Size 4.
c. Size 6.

2. When you do the Mashed Potato to your fave dance tune, does any of your flesh jiggle?
a. Flesh?
b. I suppose my earlobes are a bit weighty.
c. My breasts move up and down of their own accord.

3. At the office Christmas party, the dreamy new exec corners you under the mistletoe. Your first thought:
a. "My lips feel so incredibly fat."
b. "Can he see my knuckle fat?"
c. "I'd be so happy right now if only my vagina weren't so fat."

4. Which of the following weight-altering substances do you dig?
a. Dexies and bennies.
b. Black coffee and cigarettes.
c. Celery by the bunch.

90

5. Your bathroom scale says you've put on two and a half pounds. You:
a. Attempt suicide with your Lady Shaver.
b. Burst into tears, then rush out to buy the latest diet book, a girdle, diuretics and five different shades of Revlon contouring blush, plus some expensive perfume, two groovy suede pocketbooks, a Mary Quant outfit and fourteen pairs of go-go boots to cheer up.
c. Exercise more and eat less cheese.

INSTRUCTIONS:
1. Circle your score in each category.
2. Go back and change all of your b's and c's to a's.
3. Total your five scores, then erase your answers so your little sister can take the quiz.

1a—1	2a—1	3a—1	4a—1	5a—1
1b—2	2b—2	3b—2	4b—2	5b—2
1c—3	2c—3	3c—3	4c—3	5c—3

Your score:

5 points: Chubby Charmer
You're not *technically* overweight, according to the MetLife weight charts, but those were made in the 50s when it was okay to be *super chunky!* Says Dr. Robert Stone, author of *Your Weight Problem,* "Even if you feel happy with your body, you're still too fat. Men may date you, but not a single one will tie your knot." Don't you fret—Dr. Stone has some *good news!* "As long as you stay up-to-date on advances in dieting and cosmetics by reading beauty and fashion periodicals every month *and* buying the products they advertise, you'll soon have your pick of successful, attractive, commit-ment-minded lovers." So get crack-ing with the weight-loss pills and the contour blush, and in no time you'll be the *sexiest dollybird* on the block!

6-9 points: Portly Porker
Wow! Are you a *cow!* If you've been a loyal reader of our mag, you proba-bly feel pretty *bad* about yourself, and that's good. "Being overweight is the worst thing you can be," says Dr. Paul Grossman, author of *Yes, You Are Fat.* "Luckily, our culture keeps the pressure on fat women to slim down by emphasizing how disgust-ing they are with their out-of-control gluttony." So you've got *no excuse* for your *enormous* thighs—why not try to *shed* that hideous poundage with a combination of crash dieting, amphetamines and cigarettes? And remember that expensive makeup can work slenderizing *magic,* or at least make you believe that a *hunky hubby* might someday be within your reach, however *crazy* that might seem now!

10-15 points: Fatal Fatty
Every gal thinks she's absolutely enormous, but you really *are!* Seriously, your obesity not only can cause *health problems* but can also make you utterly *undesirable!* Author of *Oink: Make Way for Piggy!* Dr. James D. Sanford tells us, "Any woman who weighs more than 105 pounds will never get a boyfriend or a husband. That's a scientific certainty." But don't despair, Claire, 'cause there's always hope that *in another lifetime* you will be as thin and *gorgeous* as the models in our pages. If you keep subscribing to *Cosmo,* no doubt you'll get *a little bit more attractive—and* snag some sad, desperate *male member of the species* in the process! ∎

In 1969 Helen Gurley Brown, editor of *Cosmopolitan* magazine, rejected the first self-scoring reader test because it "squandered ten cover stories' worth of insecurities in one lousy quiz."

Twenty years after the first PEZ dispenser (see p. 24), the Haas Food Manufacturing Corporation began selling the dispensers in series. The company's first effort featured, from left to right, Barry Goldwater, Robert McNamara, Earl Warren, McGeorge Bundy, George McGovern, and Spiro Agnew. This series, called "Party PEZ," never made it to market, despite secret financial support from the Nixon administration.

ZZZZZZZZZ

©1968 Alphabetz, Ltd.

♂ OR ♀ Baby Names —
Barfko Swill Zappa
Why Does It Hurt When I Pee Zappa
St. Alphonzo's Pancake Breakfast Zappa
Don't Eat the Yellow Snow Zappa
Robert Urich Zappa
Zurcon Encrusted Tweezers Zappa (or just Tweezer Zappa)
Weird But Strangely Drug-Free Zappa
Torture Never Stops Zappa
Zappa! Zappa

♂ —
Willie The Pimp Zappa (Musical Talent)
I've Got My Daddy's Cock and My Mommy's Nose Zappa
Frank Zappa II (Supportive Attitude)

At first glance, the names of Frank and Gail Zappa's children, born between 1967 and 1979, may seem a bit odd: Moon Unit, Dweezil, Ahmet, and Diva Muffin. But the Zappas actually chose these names due to their conventionality, rejecting numerous others deemed too strange or controversial. When Gail suggested the possibility of an even more run-of-the-mill moniker like Henry or Linda, Frank pointed out that a child with such a name would be too likely to get confused with other children, thus heightening the possibility of a kidnapping.

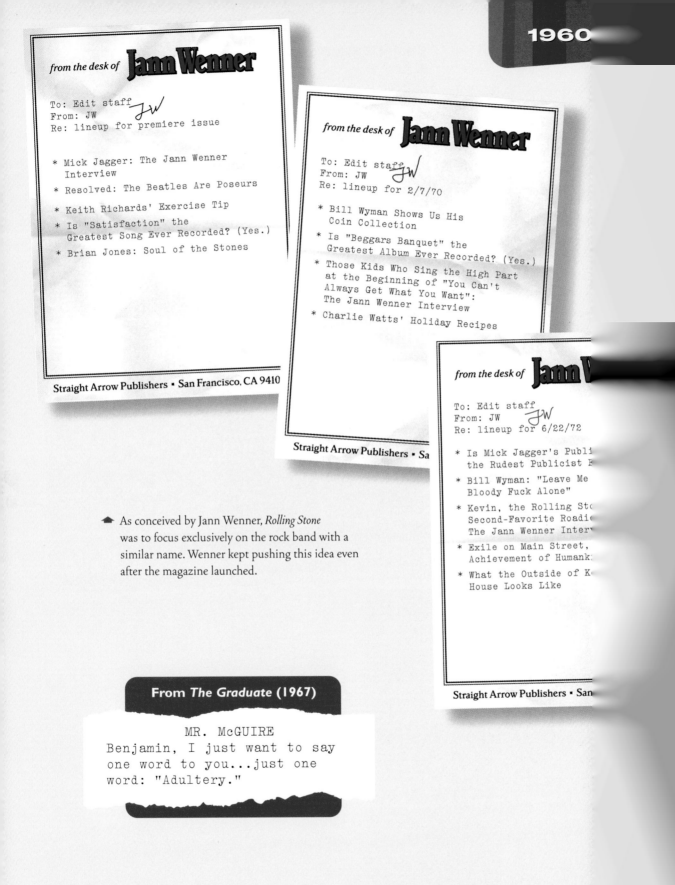

from the desk of **Jann Wenner**

To: Edit staff
From: JW
Re: lineup for premiere issue

* Mick Jagger: The Jann Wenner
  Interview
* Resolved: The Beatles Are Poseurs
* Keith Richards' Exercise Tip
* Is "Satisfaction" the
  Greatest Song Ever Recorded? (Yes.)
* Brian Jones: Soul of the Stones

Straight Arrow Publishers ▪ San Francisco, CA 9410

from the desk of **Jann Wenner**

To: Edit staff
From: JW
Re: lineup for 2/7/70

* Bill Wyman Shows Us His
  Coin Collection
* Is "Beggars Banquet" the
  Greatest Album Ever Recorded? (Yes.)
* Those Kids Who Sing the High Part
  at the Beginning of "You Can't
  Always Get What You Want":
  The Jann Wenner Interview
* Charlie Watts' Holiday Recipes

Straight Arrow Publishers ▪ Sa

from the desk of **Jann W**

To: Edit staff
From: JW
Re: lineup for 6/22/72

* Is Mick Jagger's Publi
  the Rudest Publicist I
* Bill Wyman: "Leave Me
  Bloody Fuck Alone"
* Kevin, the Rolling Sto
  Second-Favorite Roadie
  The Jann Wenner Interv
* Exile on Main Street,
  Achievement of Humank
* What the Outside of K
  House Looks Like

Straight Arrow Publishers ▪ San

🔺 As conceived by Jann Wenner, *Rolling Stone*
was to focus exclusively on the rock band with a
similar name. Wenner kept pushing this idea even
after the magazine launched.

From *The Graduate* (1967)

MR. McGUIRE
Benjamin, I just want to say
one word to you...just one
word: "Adultery."

Joan Baez, an ▶ early proponent of trucks with big tires, nearly did not perform at Woodstock after festival planners changed the event's focus.

Big Bird began Spider, a seven-longlegs. After rehearsal, all ticipants had edicated.

WOODSTOCK
CITY SPEEDWAY
in
WHITE LAKE, NY
presents

WITH
30 BIG-FOOT
MONSTER TRUCKS

SHA NA NA

RICHIE HAVENS

BURT WARD,
TV'S "ROBIN"

HOT DOGS &
BALLOONS

MUCH MORE

SUNDAY! AUGUST 10
SUNDAY! AUGUST 17
SUNDAY! AUGUST 24

3 DAYS of PEACE, MUSIC & MONSTER TRUCKS

◀ Once Mr. Spock's appearance was complete (see p. 48), the next task was to give him alien-like movements and behaviors. Leonard Nimoy came up with a special hand gesture that he could use when greeting other Vulcans. It was deemed too similar to the well-known "Call Me" gesture and replaced by fingers held in a "V."

"Don't make me angry. You wouldn't like me when I'm angry, or when I'm moderately constipated or have loose bowels, or for that matter any time I've just eaten a milk product shortly after a full meal, because it's best to wait six hours between consuming milk and consuming meat."

— Dr. David Banner in
***The Incredible Hulk* (1977)**

Chapter Three
1970-1979

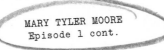

MARY TYLER MOORE
Episode 1 cont.

LOU

Look, Miss... would you please answer the questions as I
ask them.

MARY

Yes, Mr. Grant, I will but you've been asking a very lot
of personal questions that don't have a thing to do with
my qualifications for this job.

LOU

You know what you've got, kid? You've got spunk.

MARY
(looks proud of herself)

Well, yes...

LOU
(fiercely) I hate spunk.

MARY

(jumps across the desk, kicks LOU in the face)

Taste my pain, motherfucker!

◀ After Mary Tyler
Moore broke her
ankle on the set, the
series premiere and
subsequent episodes
of her eponymous
television show had
to be rewritten
without the
fight scenes.

➡ This slogan for the Ziploc plastic bag (1970)
was rejected in favor of "Perfect for packaging and
distributing cold cuts (and body parts!)"

Kermit the Frog's signature
song—"It's Not Easy Being
Green" (1970)—was
initially titled "It's Not Easy
Being a Disenfranchised
Minority Group."

SC Johnson

Ziploc®
BRAND BAGS

Perfect for
packaging and
distributing
marijuana
(and cold cuts!)

6-1/2 IN x 3-1/4 IN (16.51 CM x 8.25 CM)

This comprehensive ▶ resource on women's health and sexuality did not attract its intended audience of women.

OUR BODIES, OUR HOT WET BODIES

A Book By and For Women

By The Boston Women's Health Book Collective

◀ Instead of a wingback chair, the pilot for *All in the Family* (1971) featured Archie Bunker in a top-of-the-line massager La-Z-Boy that made him completely relaxed and extremely kind to his wife, daughter, and particularly his son-in-law, whom he called "Darling Sweethead."

In 1974 ZZ Top ▶ members Billy Gibbons and Dusty Hill decided to grow long hair on their chins rather than their heads after boxing manager Don King started copying their look.

Superstar

Every time I look at me
I don't understand
How such brilliant genius comes
From one little man
Couldn't make more money
If I'd had it planned
Amazing Technicolor Dreamcoat—
Who's not a fan?

Andrew Lloyd
Superstar
With this cheap formula
I'll go far
One torch song
and two good hooks
Stories I swiped out of others' books

Andrew Lloyd
Superstar
With this cheap formula I'll go far
Andrew Lloyd
Superstar
(Repeat throughout show)

The Trotten Horse Pub

◀ After *Joseph and the Amazing Technicolor Dreamcoat* became a hit, Andrew Lloyd Webber was so pleased that he wrote an entire rock opera about Andrew Lloyd Webber. He thought better of it in the morning and changed all of the references to Jesus Christ, who seemed a worthy, if flawed, substitute.

From *Love Story* (1970)

```
        OLIVER BARRETT IV
Love means never having to
say, "Wow, it must really suck
to have cancer."
```

Abbie Hoffman

buy this book

[Steal two of Jerry Rubin's]

◀ Until Jerry Rubin threatened to sue, Grove Press planned to use the title shown here in order to appease Abbie Hoffman, who had wanted to call his manuscript *Steal This Book, Any Other Grove Press Book, and Moon Their Offices at 743 Broadway (between 13th and 14th Streets, 1st floor), New York, NY.*

At first, the makers of this ▶ shampoo were overly conscientious about federal regulations regarding truth in personal hygiene packaging.

In 1970, a year before the Hamburglar came on the scene, Ronald McDonald's archenemy was the Hamrapist.

NET WT. 16 FL. OZ

"Gee, Your Hair Smells Like Shampoo!"

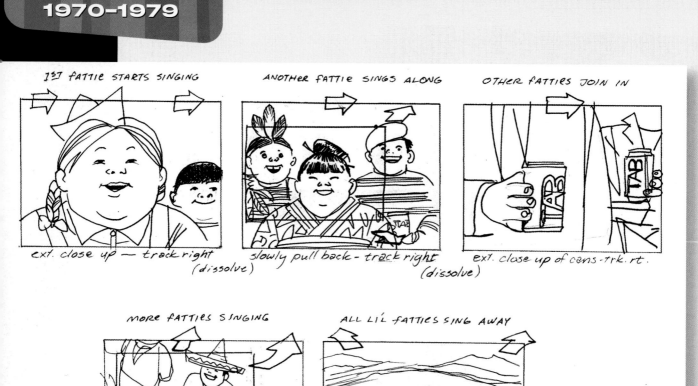

1st fattie starts singing
ext. close up — track right
(dissolve)

another fattie sings along
slowly pull back - track right
(dissolve)

other fatties join in
ext. close up of cans - trk. rt.

more fatties singing
cont. track right — crane away
(dissolve)

all li'l fatties sing away
crane away to wide shot

⬆ Coca-Cola liked this ad concept so much that the company wound up using it for Coke instead of the less-popular diet drink Tab. Despite the campaign's enduring popularity, executives still regret losing the jingle's original lyrics: "I'd like to teach the world to sing/And count each calorie/I'd like to buy the world a Tab/And death to Pepsi Free."

Programmers at ▶ Atari, concerned that Pong (1972) might be too difficult for less coordinated players, experimented with a slightly larger, easier-to-hit "ball."

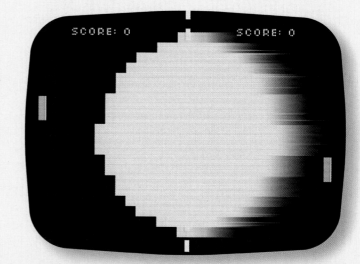

445-08431-175

$1.75

Hunter S. Thompson
author of **Hell's Angels**

Hugs AND LAUGHTER in LAS VEGAS

No cocaine, marijuana, heroin, quaaludes, speed, LSD, PCP, opium or prescription painkillers. Just Ecstasy. Pure Ecstasy.

Hunter S. ⬆ Thompson's 1971 account of a trip to Las Vegas on the newly discovered drug Ecstasy was, in the words of his editors, "so incredibly boring." They sent him back with a lifetime supply of methamphetamine to give him the anger, paranoia and boundless ego necessary to write bestsellers.

PART ONE

We were somewhere around Barstow on the edge of the desert when the Ecstasy began to take hold. I remember saying something like, "You're such a wonderful guy; maybe you would enjoy having the chance to drive . . ." and suddenly there was a sort of happy flitting noise all around us and the sky was full of butterflies, all fluttering and darting around the car, which was going about 100 miles an hour with the top down. And a voice (me) was shouting, "Pretty! Pretty!"

Then it was quiet again. My attorney was looking out toward the desert with a somewhat manic air. "What's pretty? Where? That cow skull? You're right—that's the coolest thing I've ever seen! Thanks for pointing it out. You're the best." He turned and smiled at me, vigorously rubbing his palms against my suede jacket for its incredibly cool texture.

We were on our way to cover the fabulous Mint 400 for a rave-culture magazine, which had provided us with this huge red Chevy convertible. That was nice of them, they didn't have to do that. They had also given me $300 in cash, most of which was spent on drugs. The trunk of the car looked like a car trunk filled with drugs—but the best car trunk filled with drugs ever! Yay! We had two bags of Ecstasy, seventy-five pellets of Ecstasy, five sheets of high-powered Ecstasy, a salt-shaker half full of Ecstasy and a whole galaxy of multicolored Ecstasy, E, MDMA, X . . . and also a quart of orange juice, a bag of Hershey's kisses and two dozen squeaky toys.

3

In the testing phase, the elastic doll Stretch Armstrong (1976) could be pulled in five different directions at once because he was anatomically correct.

➤ The Pet Rock (1975) was supposed to be part of a set that included Pet Paper and the product shown here.

Pet Scissors

chinese style

54· The Joy of Sex

In the classical treatises, remarkably like uninhibited European sex, the best thing being the delightful names given to postures—here, "Wild Geese Flying on Their Backs"—for quite ordinary positions. Main elaboration consists in various complicated mixtures of deep and shallow strokes, often in magical numbers—5 deep 8 shallow, etc. Intercourse naked, on a Chinese bed, in the open air, or on the floor. Woman treated far less as an equal in sex than in Indian erotology. Mystical schools tried to avoid ejaculation.

x position

156· The Joy of Sex

A winner for prolonged intercourse. Slow, coordinated wriggling movements will keep him erect and her close to orgasm for long periods. To switch back to other positions, either of them can sit up without disconnecting.

inversion

86· The Joy of Sex

Taking him or her head-down. She can lie down, raising her hips as shown—he stands between her legs and enters her from behind while she rests on her elbows or walks on her hands (the wheelbarrow). With orgasm the buildup of pressure in the veins of the face and neck can produce startling sensations.

◀ Until the final stages of publication, Dr. Alex Comfort insisted that his twelve-year-old neighbor Tommy Rutchings illustrate *The Joy of Sex* (1972).

Before George Carlin came u[p]
"The Seven Words You Can N[ever]
Say on TV" (1972), his stand-u[p]
routine relied on "hug," "flowe[r,"]
"baby," "laughter," "home," "A[rt,"]
and "love"—"The Seven Wor[ds You]
Can Never Say Without Smili[ng.]"

EAT THAT, BITCH!

EAT THAT, BITCH!

The board game Sorry! has been on the market since 1934, but in the early '70s lagging sales forced Hasbro to consider changing its name. The packaging shown here was rejected due to concern that young boys would experience gender dysphoria.

Roman Polanski convinced screenwriter Robert Towne to turn this short film into a 131-minute thriller.

```
                              CHINATOWN
                                 By
                            Robert Towne


FADE IN

INT. GITTES' OFFICE -- DAY

JAKE GITTES sits at his desk, staring at grainy surveillance photos.
His associates CURLY and WALSH look on.

The door opens and SOPHIE looks in.

                               SOPHIE
                A Mrs. Mulwray is here to see you.

                               GITTES

             Give me a minute.

                               WALSH
                Evelyn Mulwray? The water commissioner's
                daughter? Talk about your freak shows!

Curly snickers.

                               GITTES
             What are you getting at?

                               WALSH
             You don't know? Her old man knocked her up
             and she had his kid.

                               GITTES

             That's sick!

                               CURLY
                Forget it, Jake -- let's order lunch from
                Chinatown.


FADE OUT

CREDITS
```

Vanguard FILMS PRODUCTION

Lou, you crazy fuck! —

Man, I love this title: "Deep Throat."

Question: what exactly does she have in the back of her throat that gives her such pleasure when doing her thing? I've come up with a few possibilities:

o a generous amount of pubic hair
o an anus
o a clitoris
o a little tiny woman who's a total slut
o infected tonsils
o a French tickler
o another, smaller mouth leading to another, smaller throat
o a huge esophagus
o a monster epiglottis (the flap of tissue that covers the air passage to the lungs and that channels food to the esophagus)
o the laryngeal pharynx, which regulates the passage of air to the lungs
o the Hitachi Magic Wand (the Cadillac of vibrators)
o thick fibers of muscle and connective tissue which attach the pharynx to the base of the skull and surrounding structures

Let me know what you think.

Best,
Gerard

◀ After much brainstorming, Vanguard Films decided to give Linda Lovelace's character in *Deep Throat* (1972) a clitoris beneath her epiglottis.

Before being repackaged ▶ as a children's toy, Kenner's Sit 'n Spin was originally developed as a portable roadside sobriety test. Difficulty in cleaning vomit off its textured surface led to its discontinuation by all highway patrols (except Hartford, Connecticut, shown here).

Paul Stanley, Peter Criss, Ace Frehley, and Gene Simmons's original makeup was more in keeping with the band's full name, Sealed With A Kiss.

The use of any recording device, either audio or video, and the taking of photographs, either with or without flash, is strictly prohibited.

A BACKSTAGE CREW

MUSICAL NUMBERS

I HOPE I GET IT ....The Company
I CAN BUILD THAT ....Mike
EVERYTHING WAS POORLY DESIGNED AT THE BALLET......Dave, Kathy, Jodie
HELLO TWELVE, HELLO THIRTEEN, HELLO SOUND BOOTH ....John
ABILITY TO HANG LIGHTS: TEN; LOOKS: THREE....................Elaine
ONE (SINGULAR TECH RUN-THROUGH)........................The Company
WHAT I DID FOR DUCT TAPE ....Liz and the Company
ONE (SINGULAR TECH RUN-THROUGH): REPRISE..............The Company

fter-Theatre Dining

The unaired pi
ABC Afterschool
(1972) was a o
drama titled W
Osmond Makes

Due to a contract dispute with the International Alliance of Theatrical Stage Employees, this musical was rewritten as *A Chorus Line* (1975).

IN THIS ISSUE

Kevin Lawrence
Returns to
school, without
the lice

Janet McManus
Omelette truth
and triumph

Marshall Brown, Sr.
His team had never
made the playoffs,
until now

The Barkers
A really big
family, with
several cars

Larry Mills
(1928-1974)
The Stop 'n' Save
will never be
the same

People
weekly

March 4, 1974   35 Cents

**Mark and Donna's
Wedding**
They've (finally) set
a date, found a hall
and registered
at Gimbel's

◀ At first *People* (1974)
focused exclusively on
"regular folks."
Its editors refused to
accept that celebrities
are in fact human
beings and considered
them to be beyond the
purview of the magazine.

SONY
Betamax™
Video Tape Recorder

Submitted by
Stephen King
9/28/73

◀ Before turning to novels, a young Stephen King tried unsuccessfully to carve out a career in technical writing.

OPERATING INSTRUCTIONS

To Play a Tape

1. Insert a tape into the Betamax.™ The Betamax™ automatically turns on, as if acting of its own accord, as if, as if…no, that couldn't be. The tape automatically begins to play if the safety tab on the cassette has been removed and the Auto Play feature has been turned on.

2. If the tape isn't playing, press PLAY. PLAY and the time counter appear on the screen. Blood sprays the screen like the slaughterhouse floor after a busy day, while the Betamax™ makes gasping and choking sounds like the suck of a sump pump full of too much sewage. (For instructions on resetting the time counter, see page 9.)

3. If necessary, press TRACKING up or down on the remote or CHANNEL up or down on the Betamax™ to remove any streaks from the picture. But it won't help, as the blood continues to gush, trickling over the Betamax,™ falling to the carpet in growing pools of red. Details are on page 16.

4. Press STOP on the remote or STOP/EJECT on the Betamax™ to stop playback. The remote is located in the pile of human organs behind the couch.

5. Press REW. The Betamax™ will automatically rewind the tape if it reaches the end of the tape during playback, and in addition, a corpse—a skeleton, really, with a few moldering scraps of flesh dangling from its ribs—emerges from the back of the television set. Its decayed, worm-riddled brains explode from the back of its head in grisly gray splash. Brains dribble on the carpet like spoiled oatmeal, squirming with slugs and maggots, brains that smell like a woodchuck imploded by gassy decay in high-summer meadow. While rewinding, you can press POWER and the Betamax™ w still rewind the tape.

6. Press STOP/EJECT on the Betamax™ to eject the tape once it is complete rewound. You may insert another tape while the Betamax™ laughs the laugh witches and fools.

Bill Cosby's fascination with ▶ existentialism led to the creation of the animated character Fat Albert Camus and his trademark chant, "Hey hey hey, I reject the notion of responsibilitay." When television executives told Cosby to make Fat Albert less aware of the absurdity of human existence, the comedian settled for having one of the Cosby kids wear a knit hat pulled over his face and another speak entirely in gibberish.

The theme from the movie *M*A*S*H* (1970) was originally called "Suicide Hurts Badly."

LIFE CEREAL
1/12/72

Int. A suburban kitchen. Daytime. Medium close-up on two kids warily contemplating a box of cereal.

KID #1

What's this stuff?

KID #2

Some cereal. It's supposed to be good for you.

KID #1

Did you try it?

KID #2

I'm not gonna try it. You try it!

KID #1

I'm not gonna try it.

KID #2

Let's give it to Academy Award-winning actress and star of the upcoming major motion picture "The Poseidon Adventure" -- Shelley Winters!

KID #1

She won't eat it! She hates everything!

(They slide the bowl down the table. CUT TO: Shelley Winters, in a large fuchsia caftan, smoking a cigarette. She stubs out the cigarette into half a grapefruit and begins gingerly sampling the cereal. Soon, she is tucking into it with great abandon.)

KID #2

She likes it! Shelley Winters likes it!

(CUT TO: Shelley Winters tipping the bowl back to drink the last of the milk)

V.O.

Life Cereal. Shelley Winters likes it.

Due to a last-minute casting emergency, this version of the Life cereal commercial was scrapped. Instead three-year-old John Gilchrist appeared as Mikey, which led to his long and successful career in urban legends.

From *Dirty Harry* (1971)

HARRY CALLAHAN
I know what you're thinking. Did he fire six shots or only five? Well, to tell you the truth, in all this excitement, I've kinda lost track myself. In fact, I've been forgetting a lot of stuff lately. Did he turn off the oven? Does he know where he put his keys? I've completely lost track. Please don't tell the chief, but my doctor even mentioned early-onset Alzheimer's.

bell

6/23/71

Hi Marlo--

I love the album as is, but the top brass up my ass wants to see some changes. As much as hate to admit it, I think we can make the Man happy and still get our message across.

Cover design:
* Change the kids' uniforms to fashions of the privileged--jeans, t-shirts, ponytails
* Remove Mao's credit

Some songs need to be revamped as follows:

New Title as Dictated by Mgt.	Your Title
Parents Are People (People With Children)	Capitalists Are People (People Who Control the Means of Production)
Dudley Pippin	Dudley Pippin and the Petit Bourgeois
When We Grow Up	When We Fulfill Our Historical Imperative
Ladies First	Bosses First
It's All Right to Cry	It's All Right to Strike
Atalanta	Emma Goldman
Dudley Pippin and the Principal	Dudley Pippin and His Menshevik Friend
Untitled	The Internationale

Marlo, please let me know if any of this is a no-can-do.

In solidarity,

Richard T. Cooke
Vice President, Children's Music

In the pilot episode of *Happy Days* (1974), the Fonz was a lesbian.

Although Marlo Thomas agreed to the changes stipulated above, she and her record label had a similar battle over the album's 1987 sequel, *Free to Be a Family*, which Thomas wanted to call *Free to Be Three Kids, Two Women Who Love Women, Three Dads Who Have Visitation Rights, and a Dog.*

MARLO THOMAS AND FRIENDS

ALAN ALDA • HARRY BELAFONTE • MEL BROOKS • JACK CASSIDY
DICK CAVETT • CAROL CHANNING • MAO TSE TUNG • ROSEY GRIER
SHIRLEY JONES • BOBBY MORSE • THE NEW SEEKERS
DIANA ROSS • DIANA SANDS • TOM SMOTHERS

FREE TO BE... YOU AND ME

DATE: 4/18/76
TO: Fred Silverman, Chief of Programming, ABC
FROM: Larry Gelbart
RE: Treatment, "One's Company"

Summary:
Jack Tripper is a lonely bachelor and a compulsive masturbator. The only landlord who will accept him is Stanley Roper, a sour misanthrope who will not allow any "self-abuse" under his roof. But how can Jack control himself when Janet and Chrissy, his two sexy neighbors, walk around wearing next to nothing and can be easily observed through the peephole Jack drilled between their apartments?

Sample episodes:

* Jack buys a pet gerbil to keep him company. Mr. Roper hears the squeaking of the gerbil's exercise wheel and mistakes it for the sound that the springs in Jack's mattress make when Jack masturbates in bed. Where will Jack hide his pet when Mr. Roper comes calling? We think you'll be surprised.

* Jack's friend Larry develops a crush on Chrissy after spying on her from Jack's apartment. When he asks her out on a date, though, Larry's got a lot of explaining to do after he accidentally mentions the heart-shaped birthmark on her left buttock and what a coincidence it is that they both own the same vibrator.

* When Janet and Chrissy argue over who killed their spider plant, Jack shouts in falsetto through the thin walls in order to escalate their feud, hoping they will end up in a hot girl-on-girl wrestling match.

◀ Fred Silverman advised Larry Gelbart to rewrite this treatment as *Three's Company* (1977) with the following comment: "Sure, masturbation makes good TV, but a threesome constantly hinted at but never realized is ratings magic."

The celebrity host of the first episode of *The Muppet Show* (1976) was supposed to be David Crosby, but the combination of a fifth of whiskey, 1.8 grams of cocaine, two hits of LSD, a talking frog, a pig in a karate outfit, and a pair of old men making terrible puns proved to be too much for him.

A L I E N

In space, no one can
hear you scream,
unless they are in the
same spaceship with you,
in which case they can hear you,
but they can't *help* you.

TWENTIETH CENTURY-FOX PRESENTS **A L I E N**

TOM SKERRITT SIGOURNEY WEAVER VERONICA CARTWRIGHT HARRY DEAN STANTON
JOHN HURT IAN HOLM & YAPHET KOTTO AS PARKER

EXECUTIVE PRODUCER RONALD SHUSETT PRODUCED BY GORDON CARROLL, DAVID GILER AND WALTER HILL DIRECTED BY RIDLEY SCOTT
STORY BY DAN O'BANNON & RONALD SHUSETT SCREENPLAY BY DAN O'BANNON MUSIC JERRY GOLDSMITH PANAVISION® EASTMAN KODAK COLOR®

PRINTS BY DELUXE | MOTION PICTURE SOUNDTRACK AVAILABLE ON 20TH CENTURY-FOX RECORDS & TAPES |

◆ Initially, director
Ridley Scott
wanted the tag
line for *Alien*
(1979) to be
factually accurate.

Concer
Haley's
of a blac
commis:
the *Roo*
about a
Connec
by Pete
efforts t
tree tak
to Muni
to pron

The pitcher of Kool-Aid that ▶
smashes through walls when
thirsty children call originated in
1975 as a Kool-Aid packet that slips
under doors unannounced and
sprays powder everywhere. In test
screenings, this ad frightened
children and was never aired.

KOOL-AID SPOT

Girl (V.O.): "Gosh, I'm thirsty."
In B.G., Kool-Aid packet slides
under door.

Packet leaps up. "YEAHHH!"
Screaming children try to escape
but packet blocks only door.

V.O.: "E
You're th
out loud,
your thir
wherever
and meta
Kool-Aid

Before Australian ▶ Olivia Newton-John was cast in the movie version of *Grease* (1978), the lead roles were Danny, an American student who has just returned from backpacking in Bulgaria, and Sandinkia, an Olympic athlete he met while abroad. These lyrics for "Summer Nights" were scrapped when Newton-John proved unable to pull off an authentic Bulgarian accent.

```
Summer Nights

Danny:       Summer loving, had me a blast
Sandinkia:   Summer loving, happen so fast
D:           Met a girl who benched more than me
S:           Meet a boy who call me "commie"
Together:    Summer sun
             Iron Curtain fun
             Then uh oh those summer nights!

Girls:       Tell me more, tell me more
             Did he buy your TV?
Boys:        Tell me more, tell me more
             Will she ever be free?

S:           He come to flat, we share the bed
D:           I told her that Communism was dead
S:           We go to gym, I lift 415
D:           She clean-and-jerked, you know what I mean!
Together:    Summer sex
             With a Marxist complex
             But uh oh those summer nights!

Girls:       Tell me more, tell me more
             Is defection that hard?
Boys:        Tell me more, tell me more
             Does she have a green card?

             (slower)
S:           Tanks rolling in, people looting the stores
D:           I had to run back to Western shores
S:           No time for kiss or say him adieu
D:           Wonder if she died in the coup

Together:    Summer's done
             Ideology won
             But oh those summer niiiiiights!

All:         Tell me more, tell me more, tell me mooooore!!!
```

Please Pardon
the Interruption,
but We Would Like to
Take a Moment of Your Time
to Introduce You to a Group
of Fine Young Men Who
Call Themselves The
SEX PISTOLS.

Thank You.

◀ Although this cover had sold well in England, Malcolm McLaren worried that "Americans won't buy it without common, rude slang" and changed the title to *Never Mind the Bollocks, Here's the Sex Pistols* (1977).

Before they were added to the *Superfriends* lineup in 1977, the Wonder Twins were the Wonder Sextuplets: Zan could take any form of water; Jayna, any type of animal; Retal, any variety of houseplant; Looshoo, any diacritical mark; Ragat, any form of burrito, enchilada or quesadilla; and Pimto, any character from *Laverne and Shirley*.

Did you know that the grizzly bear can swim much faster than humans? Prepare to learn this.

PAWS

ROY
SCHEIDER

ROBERT
SHAW

RICHARD
DREYFUSS

PAWS

Co-starring LORRAINE GARY · MURRAY HAMILTON · A ZANUCK/BROWN PRODUCTION
Screenplay by PETER BENCHLEY and CARL GOTTLIEB · Based on the novel by PETER BENCHLEY · Music by JOHN WILLIAMS
Directed by STEPHEN SPIELBERG · Produced by RICHARD D. ZANUCK and DAVID BROWN · A UNIVERSAL PICTURE **PG** PARENTAL GUIDANCE

COPYRIGHT ©1975 BY UNIVERSAL PICTURES COUNTRY OF ORIGIN U.S.A.

In the original treatment for what became *The Bionic Woman* (1976), tennis pro Jaime Sommers sustains a head injury that robs her of the ability to say one thing while meaning the opposite. After a team of scientists replace the damaged parts of her brain with tiny machines, Sommers uses her superhuman biting wit on behalf of the government. She is the Ironic Woman.

Despite the presence of eleven bear trainers on the set, the star of *Paws* bit Richard Dreyfuss on the nipple, really hard. For insurance purposes, the grizzly's scenes had to be reshot using a mechanical shark.

Alka-Seltzer tested an ad that covered the entire process of obtaining and administering the antacid in hopes of developing partnerships with car dealers, locksmiths, and onomatopoeists.

"Step, step, k-chunk, vroom, honk, honk, k-chunk, step, step, step, whoosh, step, hmmm, step, k-ching, k-ching, step, step, k-chunk, vroom, screech, k-chunk, step, step, step, jingle, jingle, clunk, click, slam, scuff, scuff, scuff, step, step, crinkle, crinkle, gurgle, gurgle, plop, plop, fizz, fizz, oh, what a relief it is."

Alka-Seltzer.
For upset stomach and headache, gulp, gulp, gulp, burp, aaaaah.
Read the label, use only as directed.
Alka-Seltzer Miles Laboratories, Inc.

PLAYBOY INTERVIEW: JIMMY CARTER

The details of Jimmy Carter's history are common knowledge by now, and the winding path he took from peanut farmer to presidential candidate has already been mapped out many times. But there is one question the public may still not know the answer to: Who is Jimmy Carter?

When Carter agreed to our request for an interview, we made a vow to challenge him to reveal more tha...

... *force him*

PLAYBOY: A... the campaign... little numb... instance, ha... speech over...

CARTER: So... can find so... about a parti... it's a man w... starting to c... child who m... want to help... tiful woman... directly to th... I'll even tal... after a speech... phone numbe... me going.

PLAYBOY: Ev... bly emphasiz... different audi... case, there's b... cism that you... faces, that you... all people. Ho... that?

CARTER: I thin... can be with p...

PLAYBOY: Do you hope to reassure people with this interview, people who are uneasy about your religious beliefs, who wonder if you're going to make a rigid, unbending President?

CARTER: I do. Because I'm not rigid—except when it counts. Then I am rock hard. But I am human. I am human and I am tempted.

For instance, I have lusted in my heart after those bitches, you know the ones, they've got their miniskirts right up to their ass and their nipples pointing straight through their T-shirts, man, I just want to grab them and throw them on the floor and fuck them all night till they finally know what pleasure is, because let me tell you, you ain't had pleasure till you've had Jimmy pleasure. That's right. You know what I'm talkin' about.

Christ said, "I tell you that anyone who looks on a woman with lust has in his heart already committed adultery." So that's why, as soon as I feel that lust, I figure I might as well get the pussy if I've already committed the sin, if you see where I'm coming from. And God forgives me for that. Because that's what God does. It's a pretty fucking sweet deal, if you ask me.

Christ also said, "Don't consider yourself better than someone else because one guy screws a whole bunch of women behind his wife's back while the other only screws one woman behind his wife's back because he's not that great a lover and he just can't get more women to fuck him." I do not look down on men who cannot leave their women screaming into their pillow as they're being pounded from behind, the way I can.

Now let me tell you something about cunnilingus.

(Continued on page 317)

... out of ... ave been ... nportant ... paign. Is ... en have ... re cam-... es, and ... women ... of my ... wn, up ... dicated ... anoth-... ld have ... As the ... tor rose ... l ques-... elivered ... ile his ... at his ... led to ... ng, to ... t, or ... it is

"I remember one woman who told me about sexual discrimination that she had suffered, and she really touched me personally. Very personally, if you know what I mean."

"I can't change the teachings of Christ. Christ said, 'Do unto others as you would have them do unto you.' And I want others to perform oral sex on me."

"My dick is huge, I mean huge."

53

Originally Garfield (1978) was not a cat, but a fat, lazy man who liked lasagna and sponged off a hopeless bachelor named Jon.

Fantasy Island (1977) began as *Insane Delusion Island*.

Apple Computer was first conceived during an eve-of-prom suicide pact, signed in blood by Steve Jobs and Steve Wozniak: "If neither of us has gotten laid by 1976, we'll invent a user-friendly computer system, thereby turning the rest of the world into supernerds like us."

seventeen.

Dear 11-year-old girl,

Six years from now, you're going to have a lot of exciting things going on: boyfriends, eye shadow, shaving your legs, pimples, shopping, getting into the right college and anorexia. Get a head start on confronting the issues that matter, for only $6.95 a year!

Let's face it--your other sources for information just aren't adequate. Eavesdropping on your big sister's phone calls has been nearly impossible since she heard you breathing on the downstairs extension. And her diary? She's hidden it so well that even she can't find it.

Every month Seventeen magazine tells you what you'll need to know. You'll get:

- In-depth quizzes to determine whether the boy who will be in your trigonometry class in six years has a crush on you.
- Expert advice on learning to drive stick, applying lip bleach and lowering your guy's prom-night expectations, gently.
- Juicy interviews with male celebrities who would be arrested if they so much as laid a hand on you.

And so much more news you can use when you get to be a junior in high school.

All this for only 58 cents an issue. Just 58 cents--what better way to spend your milk money? Put down that teddy bear and subscribe today!

Sincerely,

Bonnie Nevins
Bonnie Nevins
Editor in Chief

Motel California

Exit 5 on the turnpike
Warm wind in my hair
Strong smell of bus exhaust
Rising up through the air
Up ahead in the distance
Neon sign flashin' bright
My head grew heavy and
    my sight grew dim
I had to stop for the night
Credit cards? They don't take 'em
I rang the office bell
Thought while looking 'round the dump
This could be Hell or this could be Hell
I took the key from Harold
But he had something to say:
"You can check out any time you like
But you'll get charged
          for the whole day."

Welcome to the Motel California
It's a dismal place
With a parking space
Lumpy twin bed at the
          Motel California
Broken ice machine
But at least it's clean.

After receiving this 1976 draft of a direct-mail solicitation, the publisher of *Seventeen* magazine fired Bonnie Nevins for being "too damn honest."

When Don Henley cowrote "Motel California," the other Eagles demanded a rewrite and a new title because the lyrics didn't contain the word "colitas."

Stevie Rubell's
STUDIO 53

milk and nilla wafer bar

Lassie blanket covers whole club

loveseat

cushions

GUEST LIST:

COUCH

radio (only Steve can touch)

Jack

Curtis

Tom

~~Julie~~

cooties

flashlights

Buzz

VIP room

main entrance

Bouncer:

VIP entrance

CUSHIONS

glue sniffers

Timmy

All others must wait and pay!!!

RULES

Look **good.**
Play **nice.**
Don't **pee.**

Nineteen years before he opened Studio 54, Steve Rubell, a Brooklyn fourth grader, managed to attract all of the popular kids from the entire borough to Studio 53 at 488 Flatbush Ave., Apt. 9E. After eight months of packed flashlight parties, the club was shut down for misuse of allowance and household chore evasion.

For budget reasons, Woody Allen's *Manhattan* (1979) was very nearly *Toronto*.

The shape of Farrah Fawcett-Majors' nipples on this poster was meant to change in direct relation to the temperature in the room, becoming more and more pronounced as the temperature dropped. The prototype proved too costly.

"Luke ... I am your cousin."

— Darth Vader in *The Empire Strikes Back* (1980)

Chapter Four
1980–1989

During the making of her first album, Madonna rejected these wardrobe designs and many others before selecting the Over-Accessorized Thrift-Store Slut look.

WARNER BROS. **WB** RECORDS INC.

Carl--   6/23/82

Enclosed is a color Xerox of some new sketches our art department has worked up for Ms. Ciccone, who, incidentally, prefers to be called "Madonna." I hate to rush you, but we need to come to a decision soon about her look -- at this rate we're going to end up sending her out in her underwear.

Mark Coyne
Artists & Repertoire

1. MAORI WARRIOR
2. HOT DOG ON A STICK CASHIER
3. MORK
4. POPEYE

3300 Warner Boulevard, Burbank, CA 91505

Before shortening this ▶ slogan, Calvin Klein considered this alternative: "Nothing comes between me and my Calvins, except the knowledge that, ultimately, every human being is alone."

"Nothing comes between me and my Calvins, except the thin layer of air molecules that exists between any two solids, no matter how close they are."

When *The Smurfs* television show (1981) was first proposed to Hanna-Barbera, the first twelve episodes directly followed the plot of Thomas Pynchon's novel *The Crying of Lot 49*.

Calvin Klein Jeans

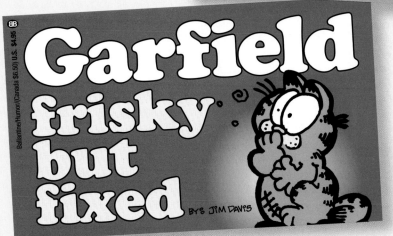

◀ For fear of offending castratos, eunuchs, and his own cat, Jim Davis changed the title of his first compilation of Garfield comics to *Garfield at Large* (1980).

Although now famous for his "I don't get no respect" shtick, Rodney Dangerfield was still trying to find his comedy niche as late as 1980, as shown in these notes.

Before latching onto aerobics, Jane Fonda tried to cash in on the high-IQ craze that swept the country between April 2 and April 6, 1981.

KARL **K** VIDEO

WORKOUT

Starring Jane Fonda

A Complete Three-Part Mental Workout:

Beginner, Advanced and Supergenius

Features:

spatial reasoning warm-ups

imaginary number crunches

Xeno's paradox (low impact)

I tell you, I am very well respected. I had sex with my wife the other night, she said, "That was wonderful. You're a very attentive lover."

I went to a hooker the other day, she told me she had a headache. But luckily I had some aspirin. A half hour later she felt well enough to have sex with me.

I was a very good looking kid. My dad took me to the zoo, and they said, "Hey, your kid's very good looking!"

I get lots of respect, lots of respect. My wife, she likes to talk during sex. The other night, she called me from a motel room. And she said, "I've rented this motel room, come have sex with me." And I did. And she talked all the way through it. And one of the things she said was that she was very satisfied with both my performance and the size of my penis.

SOUND OF AXE, THEN JACK:
"DY-NO-MITE!"
OR "SIT ON IT!"
OR "DA PLANE, DA PLANE!"
OR "WHATCHOO TALKIN' 'BOUT
    WILLIS?"
OR "IT'S 'THE MUPPET SHOW',
WITH OUR VERY SPECIAL GUEST,
MISS BERNADETTE PETERS!"
(JACK WAGGLES ARMS IN THAT
DISTINCTIVE KERMIT-LIKE WAY)

➤ Decades before Trump Tower, Trump Plaza, and Trump Taj Mahal, nine-year-old Donald experimented with naming his belongings after himself, such as the Trump Pants (shown here) and the Trump Blanky.

In 1985 a coalitio
called USA for Af
Are the World" t
starving children.
group called itself
raised money for
bers of the group
of the Moment." I
charity sponsored
the album *Final Co*
the name USA fo
organization was
as USA for Kansa
Chicago, and USA

The beer industry used its clout to convince NBC that a show set in a bar would be even funnier than the premise for *Cheers* (1982) outlined here.

October 12, 1981

Brandon Tartikoff
President of Entertainment, NBC
452 Beverly Dr.
Burbank, CA 90012

James L. Burrows
840 Santa Monica Blvd.
Los Angeles, CA 90004

Brandon--

Here's the idea I mentioned at dinner last week. It's my favorite of the bunch.

Cheers

Summary: "Cheers" is a situation comedy about six alcoholics who meet every night after work at Alcoholics Anonymous meetings in the lounge of the Boston Municipal Recreation Center. The Rec Center regulars laugh about their past hijinks as irresponsible drinkers and get into new pickles as introspective teetotallers. With sobriety comes hilarity.

This series will appeal to anyone who's ever had a drinking problem, or even just a two-week bender. And it has built-in longevity: 12 steps equals 12 seasons!

Characters:

Sam Malone: A former pro-baller who flirts with any recovering alcoholic in a skirt.

Coach Pantusso: Fifty-eight-year-old Coach dried out a little too late, but his addled thoughts are both charming and incomprehensible.

Diane Chambers: The reigning expert on AA methods and procedures, this blonde is not afraid to show it, especially to Sam! If she should leave to pursue a career in movies unexpectedly, she can be replaced by a brunette or a Scientologist, or both.

Carla Tortelli: A devoted single mother of eleven, Carla misses the sharp witticisms that flowed out of her as the liquor flowed in.

Cliff Clavin: Previously employed by the United States Postal Service, Cliff was fired after too many drunken incidents of delivering letters to the people who sent them.

Norm Peterson: Norm's humorously enormous girth is matched only by his newfound faith in a higher power.

Dr. Frasier Crane: To be introduced as the series develops and the other characters die of cirrhosis. The only member of the group with an actual doctorate in drinking, Frasier will eventually be spun off into a series of popular rehab hospitals.

I'm still working on the pilot, but here's what I have so far: The gang is tying one on in a bar called Cheers--falling off stools, making loud, lewd remarks, etc. Soon the fists start flying, and Norm's hand goes through a plate glass window. Meanwhile, Carla accuses Cliff of ruining her life, and Sam and Diane have drunken sex in the ladies' room that they'll forget in the morning.

Now all I have to do is get them to AA. Any ideas? Let's talk.

Jim

SOOTHE THE PLANET

Soft Rock CAFE

AIR SUPPLY

CHUCK MANGIONE

THANKS FOR RELAXING AT...

JAMES TAYLOR

Amy Heckerling's first feature was supposed to be *Fast Times at the Ridgemont Learning Annex.*

◆ At the Soft Rock Café, which opened in the U.S. in 1981 and closed within a month, the waiters and waitresses were trained to read the specials slowly and soothingly, "easy listening style."

Certain scenes from ▶ the "Just Say No" episode of *Diff'rent Strokes* had to be retaped multiple times, all for the same reason.

NBC: Proud as a Peacock!
National Broadcasting Company
STANDARDS AND PRACTICES DIVISION

SCENES B, F AND G NEED
TO BE RE-SHOT, AS MR.
COLEMAN IS VISIBLY AROUSED.
THANKS, JL

UCA60
Videocassette

PROGRAM: DIFF'RENT STROKES

GUEST STAR: NANCY REAGAN

TO AIR: 4/23/83

Made in USA

The climactic ▶
scene in
*The Empire
Strikes Back*
(1980) as first
envisioned by
George Lucas.

PROPERTY OF
LUCASFILM
Ltd

TOP SECRET
THE EMPIRE STRIKES BACK
First Draft -- 4/7/79
Writers: GL, LB, LK

INT. GANTRY - OUTSIDE CONTROL ROOM - REACTOR SHAFT

Luke moves along the railing and up to the control room.

Vader lunges at him and Luke immediately raises his lit sword to meet Vader's.
Sparks fly as they duel, Vader gradually forcing Luke backward toward the
gantry.

                              VADER
          It is useless to resist. Don't let yourself be destroyed as
          Obi-Wan did.

Vader's sword comes down across Luke's right forearm, cutting off his hand and
sending his sword flying.

                              VADER
          You have only begun to discover your power. Join me and I will
          complete your training. With our combined strength, we can end
          this destructive conflict and bring order to the galaxy.

                              LUKE
          I'll never join you!

                              VADER
          You must. It is your destiny. Luke... I am your cousin.

Shocked, Luke looks at Vader in utter disbelief.

                              LUKE
          No. No. That's not true! That's impossible!

                              VADER
          Search your feelings. You know it to be true.

                              LUKE
          No! No! No!

                              VADER
          Your father Anakin had an aunt. Do you remember Pi-Lippa?

                              LUKE
          You're Pi-Lippa's son? It can't be! No!

                              VADER
          No, no. I'm not Pi-Lippa's son. Pi-Lippa married Adi Gallia of
          Coruscant. Did you ever meet Adi?

                              LUKE
          No. I don't understand.

In the pilot episode of *Knight Rider*
(1982), K.I.T.T. frequently asks
Michael to stroke the gear shift.
"May I request, Michael, that in
the future you squeeze me a bit
harder—ah, yes—now a bit faster..."

Instead of Eliot luring E.T. into his house with a trail of Reese's Pieces, the original script had E.T. lapping up a trail of Miracle Whip.

Luke moves back along the gantry to its extreme end. Vader follows. There is nowhere else to go.

VADER

Adi Gallia has a cousin named Boss Nass of Otoh Gunga, whose son, Bossk--now a noted reptilian Trandoshan bounty hunter-- married a musician named Rystáll.

LUKE

Doesn't she play in the Max Rebo Band?

VADER

Exactly. I think they're playing Endor this weekend.

LUKE

I can't make it, I got a thing.

Luke makes a quick move around the instrument complex attached to the end of the gantry. Vader's sword comes slashing down, cutting the complex loose.

VADER

Anyhoo, Rystáll's older brother Grand Moff Tarkin and his companion Wedge Antilles adopted a young boy many years ago. That boy was…

LUKE

Don't say it. It can't be you. It can't!

VADER

No, it was Walrus Man, now a Galactic senator and supreme leader of the Rebel Alliance. But Walrus Man is my brother.

LUKE

NOOOO!!!!!

VADER

Join me, and together we can rule the galaxy as second cousin and second cousin.

LUKE

Don't you mean first cousins twice removed?

VADER

Are you sure? I never could get that straight. Either way, you have to admit it's a good plan.

Vader puts away his sword and holds his hand out to Luke.

A calm comes over Luke, and he makes a decision. In the next instant he steps off the gantry platform into space. The Dark Lord looks over the platform and sees Luke falling far below.

VADER
(shouting after him)
See you at Thanksgiving, then!

After this suction-cup Garfield caused several major traffic accidents, Dakin Inc. tried to develop a see-through version but settled for making the plush toy much smaller.

Bright Lights, Small City
By Jay McInerney

Chapter One

You are not the kind of guy who would be at a place like this after 10 pm. But here you are, and you cannot say that the terrain is entirely unfamiliar, although the details are fuzzy. You are at a club talking with a girl with a mullet. The club is either the Rotary or the VFW. All might become clear if you could just slip away to the snack bar and have another Mountain Dew. Then again, it might not, since Mountain Dew contains caffeine, which sometimes makes you jittery.

Jay McInerney's editors felt that his original manuscript lacked important literary elements like models and cocaine, so he rewrote it as *Bright Lights, Big City* (1984).

Laser Tag began as a competition for ophthalmologists called Laser Eye Surgery Tag.

UBU PRODUCTIONS

"Sit, Ubu, Sit!"

December 6, 1981

To: Brandon Tartikoff
From: Gary David Goldberg

Brandon--

I've been considering NBC's lineup, and I think I've got the sitcom you need post-Cosby: "A Family's Ties," a show told from the point of view of a bright, sensitive 11-year-old girl named Jennifer Keaton. She's coping with all the things that a child has to deal with on the cusp of junior high: self-esteem issues, puberty, the push-and-pull of parental and sibling relationships. I haven't fleshed out the other characters--obviously, she will have parents and some siblings (maybe a sweet but dim-witted brother and a smart-aleck sister)--but the core of the show is going to be Jennifer, her life and her experiences.

And I've already found my Jennifer: Last week I met an utterly charming young actress who I'm convinced has the chops to become a major star. Brandon, you and I must introduce America to its next superstar: Miss Tina Yothers.

Call me.

Best,

In 1982 NBC executives thought they had a hit and a breakout star in *Family Ties* (1982). They were right, sort of.

Cabbage Patch Adults ▶
didn't get past the focus
group stage because
the dolls reminded
people too much of family
members they dislike.

Cabbage Patch Adults

*All they want is love and
financial support and to be
adopted into a home like yours
so they can lie around and watch TV.*

**PLEASE
HIT THE
OTHER
CARS**

◀ This sign eventually became "Baby on
Board" (1985), a message that radically
improved driving conditions on the
nation's highways. Aggressive, drunk,
and incompetent drivers were shocked
into better behavior by the thought of
a car with a baby in it.

Robert Urich was the first choice to play Punky Brewster. The star of fifteen television shows in the course of his career, Urich was also the first choice to play Matlock, Alex P. Keaton on *Family Ties*, Benny Stulwicz on *L.A. Law*, Lacey on *Cagney & Lacey*, J.R. on *Dallas*, Webster, the robot girl from *Small Wonder*, and Homer Simpson.

From *Bull Durham* (1988)

```
            CRASH DAVIS
Well, I believe in the soul, the
woman's back, the hanging curve b
fiber, the fact that one can only
in one's life by submitting to Al
I believe Allah is the proper name
God, and I believe He is without
without end, and He alone sees ar
things. I believe Allah alone is
it is He alone that deserves our
and worship. I believe in five pr
fasting, almsgiving and I believe
the pilgrimage to Mecca during th
Hajj. [pause] Salaam alaykum.
```

FRANKIE SAY WASH THIS SHIRT IN COLD WATER, TUMBLE DRY LOW HEAT DO NOT IRON

2-LITER

New
Coke
Trade-mark ®

Frankie changed his advice to "Relax, don't do it," another bit of wisdom he got from his mother.

The first recipe for New Coke (1985) consisted solely of milk and orange juice.

From *Dirty Dancing* (1987)

JOHNNY CASTLE
Nobody puts Baby in a corner.
Babies need constant attention
for their emotional and physical
well-being.

ALL I REALLY NEED TO SMEAR WITH FINGERPAINT I SMEARED WITH FINGERPAINT IN KINDERGARTEN

◇

ROBERT FULGHUM

In its vanity-press first edition, Robert Fulghum's book was a strident manifesto denouncing "the pointless and deleterious proliferation of fingerpaint, glitter, chocolate milk, and napping in adult life today."

Within a year of the death of his *Dallas* character Bobby Ewing, actor Patrick Duffy decided he wanted to return to the show, despite advances in the plot predicated on Bobby's demise. Stumped by the prospect of working Bobby back into the storyline, the *Dallas* writers held an all-night brainstorming session that resulted in this page of ideas, all of which were rejected in favor of making the entire last season a dream.

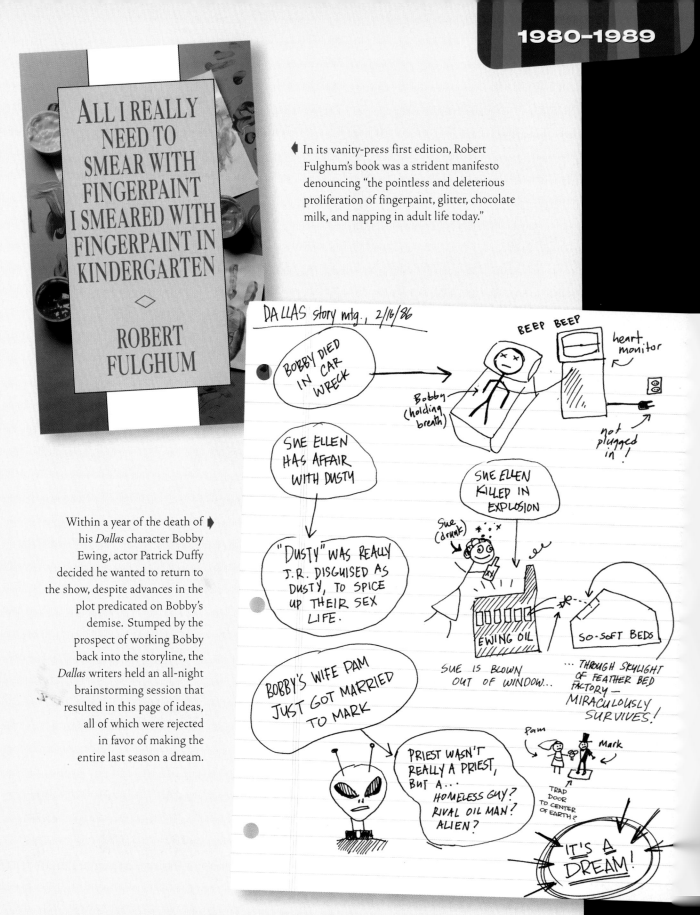

BEEF PATTY

LETTUCE

MUSTARD

BUN (TOP)

TOMATO

MAYONNAISE

BUN (BOTTOM)

PICKLE

RESTROOM KEY

CHEESE SLICE

KETCHUP

RECEIPT

◀ In 1985 McDonald's streamlined this McDLT prototype into a two-section package—one part for the hot burger, one part for the cold cheese, lettuce and tomato—which was a helpful feature for observant Jews and vegetarians on dates with meat-eaters.

In the pilot episode of *Miami Vice* (1984), Don Johnson wore socks but no shoes.

In 1987 Ben & Jerry came up with the idea of an ice cream flavor based on a counterculture hero. They swapped Jerry Orbach for Jerry Garcia when market researchers suggested that the latter would drive "pot-munchies-induced impulse sales."

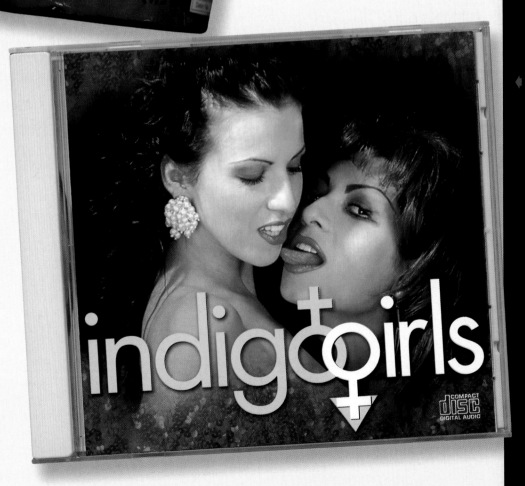

To improve the label's sales among straight men, Epic Records signed lipstick lesbians Emmanuelle and Sindi in 1986. Before the album shown here was even released, the duo broke the contract to work in adult video, making room for nonlipstick lesbians Amy and Emily.

TAPE 4B	TRACK II	DATE 4/25/86 (WW)
TITLE WALDO AT THE PARK - WHERE'S WALDO?	SND TECH: DAVIES	DEPT. VOICE-2

READER:

Here is the park. The predominant colors in this landscape are green and blue, for the grass and sky, respectively. There are three main components to the park: the pond, situated in the lower right, the playground in the upper left, and the field. In total, twenty-four trees grace the horizon between grass and sky. Some of these trees bear fruit. One of these fruits, oddly, is red with white stripes. For the most part, the rest of these fruits are clearly apples. It is the apple-picking time of year. Indeed, there are three ladders resting against three of the trees; two of them are red, one of them is white. At a quick glance, the ladders almost appear to create a red-and-white striped pattern, not unlike those found on the shirts of our hero, Waldo himself. The non-fruit bearing trees are oak and maple trees. Twenty of the trees are beginning to lose their foliage. Four coniferous trees, mainly clustered on the periphery, remain green. Those leaves remaining on the twenty deciduous trees have begun to turn yellow, orange and red; in some places, where the red leaves meet the pale sky, the red-white combination might lead one to believe that our friend Waldo is roaming in the branches of the trees. Though this is not the case, the trees and leaves will continue to be described in detail. A fair number of leaves have collected on the ground below. Most of them do not stray far from the base of the oak trees, though a good number of the leaves that have fallen from the maple trees have landed quite a distance from their respective trunks. Let us now focus on the first of the three main areas of the park: the pond. The water of the pond is an inviting blue-green. In the middle of the pond, a small island protrudes roughly three feet above the surface of the water. On this island lives a family of cross-bred birds; one of the parents is red, the other white, and three children are red with white stripes. The island levels off near its crest, forming a suitable base for a miniature lighthouse, which extends upwards to the heavens. The lighthouse, not surprisingly, is red with white stripes. At this particular instant of time, the light is pointing west. On the banks of the pond, a girl is in direct line of the light's path; she raises her red-and-white gloves to her face to shield her eyes from the novelty lighthouse's illumination. A young mother, wearing a blue shirt and embarrassingly outdated knee-high leg warmers with a red-and-white striped pattern, kneels to comfort her

Before settling on the illustrated-book format, the creators of *Where's Waldo?* (1987) produced a series of audiotapes for the blind.

child, though it is clear from the look in her eyes that she is not so much sympathetic as she is hopeful that her child might act a bit more mature and deal with the problem in a non-attention-obtaining fashion. There is a boy feeding ducks. He is wearing a red-and-white sweater, vertically striped. His father is aghast because a goose is chasing him hither and thither. The goose, it appears, is actually the parent of several young goslings which follow him in a cute style reminiscent of "Make Way for Ducklings," only with geese. The geese are neither red nor white. Let us now move our attention to the playground. Here, general chaos rules as a result of a runaway ice cream vendor cart. One child wearing red pants and a white shirt is in the act of diving out of the way of the ice cream cart, which, upon further inspection, does not sell Choco-Tacos. An ice cream sandwich is being jettisoned into the air; the wind is blowing the wrapper off, and, consequently, an attentive young girl with pigtails is waiting at the terminus of the ice cream sandwich's parabolic flight with an open mouth. The owner of the cart, employed by a company whose ubiquitous colors are white and red, is understandably distraught. He is running with arms forward, as if to clutch the handle of his beloved, estranged cart, despite the undeniable speed advantage of the cart heading down one of the field's slopes. On the jungle gym, four youngsters climb and enjoy the novelty of being high above the ground. One boy wearing a Red Sox baseball cap is sporting a white jersey and what appear to be red pajama bottoms. Three girls are grouped on the left side of the jungle gym, timidly approaching the seven-foot-high apex. Waldo is sitting on the grass underneath the jungle gym, partially obscured by the small iron bars in front of him. There is also a sandbox, crowded with too many children to count, most wearing blue. Some have pails, others shovels, as children in a sandbox are likely to have. An inexpensive pine comprises the perimeter of the sandbox, painted with a burgundy varnish donated by a goodhearted widow who co-owns the local hardware store. Two children are climbing a slide, with eager eyes. The lower of these two climbers is agitated that the one above is not climbing faster, though, really, this will not significantly affect how soon he is able to go down the slide. One child is descending the long chute, tummy down, his favorite way to enjoy the slide. His white shirt jumps out against the red, plastic slide. A handful of dutiful parents look on from the edge of the playground. One is reading a book. Three, in a small huddle, are talking about the colors red and white. They are

neither overprotective of their children nor too neglectful of their children's behavior on the playground. The field, which spans the entire scene, sports fertilized grass mowed biweekly. Two squirrels are playfully wrestling each other, evidently not aware of a nice mound of acorns not two yards away. Two boys are playing catch with a miniature Kansas City Chiefs football. Mid-spiral, this particular pass, much to the credit of the momentary quarterback, seems to be right on the money. The second boy stands ready with open arms; although, from his elbows-pinned-by-hips posture, one can only infer that he has yet to learn proper football-catching technique, which, as an American, he will undoubtedly be taught sometime in the coming years. Had the pass been a bit overthrown, the second boy might have tripped over the edge of the sandbox, just a foot or two behind him. On this day, though, the second boy is safe. Would that the same could be said for the aforementioned ice cream vendor—upon a second look, he is quite clearly panicked.

So...where's Waldo?

The answer is: Waldo is sitting on the grass underneath the jungle gym.

BUDDY HACKETT · JENNIFER GREY

Dirty Dancing

First dance.
First love.
The time of your life.

Vestron Pictures presents DIRTY DANCING · Buddy Hackett · Jennifer Grey
Also Starring: Jerry Orbach · Cynthia Rhodes · Jack Weston
Written by Eleanor Bergstein · Directed by Emile Ardolino
Filmed in Dolby Digital Sound

PG PARENTAL GUIDANCE SUGGESTED

◄ In the first version of *Dirty Dancing* (1987), Baby (Jennifer Grey) vacations at a Catskills resort with her family and falls for the camp's stand-up comic, Morrie (Buddy Hackett), from whom she must learn insult comedy and tap dancing before the summer's end. Her experience of first love is made bittersweet by class differences and by her lover's arsenal of funny voices. When Hackett was sidelined by a herniated disc halfway through filming, Patrick Swayze stepped in, and the character was rewritten to compensate for Swayze's lack of Borscht Belt flair.

From *Wall Street* (1987)

```
        GORDON GEKKO
Greedo, for lack of a better
word, is good. Greedo is right.
Greedo works. Greedo is a
bounty hunter under the employ
of Jabba the Hutt.
```

Reebok designed its ▶
Mouth Pump Sneakers on
the assumption that any
buyer of athletic gear is in
good physical condition.
After asthma sufferers,
smokers, and people
confined to iron lungs
called the sneakers
discriminatory, a tiny hand-
pump was incorporated
into the shoe.

AMERICA
Online.

Steve Case
Founder, Chairman, President

9/3/89

TO: JK, BW, LD, SG
RE: **Audio for e-mail notification**

Great meeting yesterday on the user sign-on interface
and the recorded message. I think we've got a winner:

"You've got unsolicited pornographic mail!"

Some other possibilities:
"You've got canonical lists of emoticons!"
"You've got forwarded top-ten lists!"
"You've got opportunities to make BIG BUCKS from home!"

◀ Once America Online
decided on the wording
"You've got mail," the next
step was to hire just the
right voice to record it.
Steve Case wanted Fozzie
Bear, but Frank Oz balked
at the stock-options-only
payment, forcing Case to
use Elwood Edwards, the
husband of one of his
employees.

SIDE ONE
To Live and Die in the Maze
Wonda Why They Call U Blinky
So Many Dots (Eat 'Em Up)
How Long Will
They Chase Me

SIDE TWO
I Wonder If Heaven Got a Power-up
Pac-Man Fever (xtra clean version)
Bitch Touch My Joystick
(Only When It's Your Turn)
If I Die This Level

At age seventeen,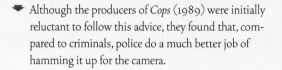
2Pac-Man Shakur not only
rapped about the video
game geek life, he lived it.

2PAC-MAN

Strictly
4 My
W.A.K.K.A.Z.

Although the producers of *Cops* (1989) were initially
reluctant to follow this advice, they found that, com-
pared to criminals, police do a much better job of
hamming it up for the camera.

FOX Legal Department
1681 San Leandro Drive
Beverly Hills, CA 90213-0900

```
10/2/88
To: Barbour/Langley Productions
Re: COPS

We agree that the footage is compelling, but
for legal reasons, perhaps the camera crew
should be riding with law enforcement rather
than with the criminals.
```

40 ACRES AND A MULE FILMWORKS

Do The Right Thing

A SPIKE LEE JOINT

INT: SAL'S FAMOUS PIZZERIA - DAY

Buggin' Out, a b-boy, is looking up at the Wall of Fame, 8 x 10 glossies of famous Italian Americans. Joe DiMaggio, Perry Como, Al Pacino, etc.

> **BUGGIN' OUT**
> Sal, how come you ain't got no brothers up on the wall here?

> **SAL**
> You open your own business, you can have your brothers, your aunts, your cousins, anybody you want. My pizzeria, my pictures.

> **BUGGIN' OUT**
> You might own this place, but rarely do I see any Italian Americans eating in here. All I see is black folks. So since we spend much money here, there should be some brothers up on the wall.

> **SAL**
> Oh, *black folks!* I thought you meant your actual brothers. There's a picture of Bill Cosby right behind you.

> **BUGGIN' OUT**
> Shit, figures it'd be the whitest black man alive.

> **SAL**
> (pointing)
> Well, there's Martin Luther King—

> **BUGGIN' OUT**
> King! White people always goin' on about—

> **SAL**
> And that's Angela Davis and Malcolm X next to her. And across the way is Kwame Ture. You may know him as civil rights activist Stokely Carmichael. Oh, and here's one of my favorites: it's a picture of me with Julian Bond at an NAACP fundraiser a few years back.

> **BUGGIN' OUT**
> Um, in that case, I'll take two slices and a Coke.

> **SAL**
> Okay, here you go. Come again!

> **BUGGIN' OUT**
> (angry)
> What the fuck did you say?

> **SAL**
> I said, "Come again."

> **BUGGIN' OUT**
> OK, thanks, I will.

He leaves.

◀ Spike Lee had to rewrite this scene in *Do the Right Thing* (1989) after Danny Aiello, who played Sal, kept mispronouncing "Kwame Ture."

Killed in Space

Christa McAuliffe
d. 1986
22 USA

Laika
d. 1957
22 USA

Obi-wan Kenobi
22 USA
d. a long time ago

◀ When the U.S. Postal Service tested this series of space program stamps among collectors, it found that philatelists would rather see a set honoring those who have been lost but not necessarily killed in space, such as Will Robinson.

Roseanne Barr

2/17/87
TO: ABC Programming
FROM: Roseanne Barr
RE: Sitcom pitch

Where are The Honeymoon
Married With Children .
kind of sitcom where a
rude, over-the-top, bu
that won't make Americ

My show will address t
violence, lesbianism,
is a life I've lived.
the ultimate complimer
I may not be blonde a
or black and skinny l
to be. I think the co
look like Shirley Par

It will be hilarious

XOXO

Roseanne Barr

enc: head shot, oth

...? And don't tell me

abc

Sounds great!
Lose the fat chick
and let's greenlight it!
T.D.

500 S. Buena Vista Street • Burbank, CA 91521

ABC commissioned a ▶ Roseanne Barr–less pilot of *Roseanne* that starred Calista Flockhart. The network reinstated Barr after studio audiences remained silent for the show's entire twenty-two minutes.

Sally leans back in ecstasy

C.U. orgasmic delight

C.U. Harry nonplussed

C.U. Harry's foot in action

In order to maintain an R-rating, Nora Ephron was forced to rewrite this scene in *When Harry Met Sally* (1989).

Chapter Five
1990-2000

Think education is expensive?
Try getting Hall and Oates to play your daughter's bat mitzvah, then we'll talk expensive.

◀ The second sentence was shortened to "Try ignorance."

The Spice Girls' original lineup: Shaped Like an Apple Spice, Asthmatic Spice, George Washington Carver Spice, Unironic "Spice," Mormon Wife #8 Spice, and Couldn't Handle the Citadel Spice.

➤ Instead of resisting the bourgeois living granted by the success of *Nevermind* (1991), Nirvana embraced it in this never-released album.

NIRVANA

HEY, ANYONE GOING TO STARBUCKS, BECAUSE IF YOU ARE, I COULD USE A HALF-CAF LATTE.

Polka!

THE PERMITTED DANCE

POLKA! THE PERMITTED DANCE · A DEUTSCH FILM GROUP PRODUCTION · HELGA SCHMIDT · HEIND SCHULTE
MUSIC BY THE RHINE POLKA ENSEMBLE AND THE BRAUNSCHWEIGER BOYS · COLOR BY CHROMOLUXE
SOUNDTRACK AVAILABLE ON HI-SOUND RECORDS AND TAPES

G | GENERAL AUDIENCES
All Ages Admitted

COURTTV

Confidential and proprietary
by Steven Brill, February 23, 1991
Brill Media Ventures, L.P.

Court TV
Executive Summary

Anybody who's served on a jury knows how tedious legal proceedings can be. The slightest distraction is a godsend. That's why I'm proposing Court TV, a network of television sets placed in courtrooms throughout America, constantly tuned to one of the three major networks—whoever offers the highest bid! By modifying the sets so the channel can't be changed, we will ensure that the given network gets its money's worth. And advertisers will love the courtroom demographic: Lawyers comprise an increasingly affluent niche that traditionally has been hard to reach. This also describes a lot of criminals.

◀ The initial business plan for Court TV (1991) did not attract investors.

MEN ARE FROM MARS,
Women Won't Shut Up

JOHN GRAY, Ph.D.

Beanie Babies ▶ (1993) were initially sold as Beanie Teens. Along with Pierce the Puppy shown here, the Ty Company offered Acne the Bear, Early Menses the Mouse, and Fuzzstache the Frog.

TOY BARN
$9.98 -TX
0 08421 04299 9

◀ John Gray may have changed the title of his 1992 bestseller, but he left its contents intact.

In the first version ▶
of *Seinfeld* (1990),
Jerry was a market
researcher, as were
Elaine, Kramer,
George, and
George's parents.

INT. JERRY'S CUBICLE - DAY

JERRY, a suitclad 30-year-old, is sitting behind his desk, talking into a phone headset. An open White Pages and a notepad lie on his desk.

                    JERRY
    What's the deal with Froot Loops? (PAUSE) No,
    seriously, what's the deal with them? (PAUSE) Have you
    ever had them? (PAUSE) Did you like them? (PAUSE) Can
    you think of improvements that would make you more
    likely to buy them again?

Jerry begins taking notes.

                    JERRY
    Mmm hmm. Mmm hmm. Please continue; this is all very
    useful.

A shorter, balding man peeks his head into the cubicle. He is GEORGE.

                    GEORGE
    Psst! Jerry!

Jerry gestures "one minute."

                    JERRY
    And would changing the color of Toucan Sam's beak—

                    GEORGE
    Jerry! Elaine got the results from the Dannon focus
    groups!

A shocked Jerry drops the headset and runs out. George creeps over and picks it up.

                    GEORGE
    (WHISPERING) Hiya, (GLANCES AT JERRY'S NOTES) Miss
    Collins? I was just, um, wondering what you think of
    sponge baths, particularly those involving Scotch-Brite-
    brand sponges. If possible, try to comment on both the
    sponge's water retention and its longevity.

While plotting out *The X-Files* (1993), Chris Carter envisioned a vast alien conspiracy orchestrated by a mysterious figure known as The Chaw-Spitting Man.

Francesca

Pungent autumn was birthday time for Francesca Johnson, and the odor of decaying leaves swept through the family room windows, reminding her deeply of the man who six years ago returned her to herself, postage due. It happened on this exact spot, this same couch, this special sofa, the preferred locale of her husband Robert's monstrously boring and conservative rear-end. This worn divan—Robert had offered to reupholster it, but she refused without explanation, mentally fingering the memories woven forever into its cushions.

> For the first *Law and Order* spinoff—*Law and Order: Special Victims Unit* (1999)—Dick Wolf envisioned a one-hour drama about cops and lawyers who struggle with the challenges of protecting the developmentally disabled.

◀ *Jeff Bridges of Madison County*, a manuscript written and designed by Robert James Waller using his Mac Classic, was rejected by a literary agent with the following note: "Women's fiction is supposed to give them something to fantasize about while having sex with their husbands. This, sir, is no women's fiction."

19
_____

Jeff Bridges of Madison County

Francesca Johnson was a farm wife with two adoring and adorable teenagers who would blanch and perhaps vomit if they knew what her heart wanted, what her heart had done to get what it wanted, what her heart had sacrificed to keep what it wanted from ruining the farm, the family, the county—she limited her ritual to once a year. Luckily the week of her birthday always coincided with the Des Moines Livestock Fiesta, and Robert and the kids couldn't miss Sheep Tuesday. Now it was Sheep Tuesday, 1991. Francesca wrapped herself in her family's absence and Jeff's imminent, thickening presence.

The rites had begun. Once started, Jeff's domination of Francesca precisely the way she wanted to be dominated would not end until she was one with him and him with her. They would form a pulsing entity that was at once prehistoric and futuristic, both pre-Darwinian and post-Freudian, simultaneously very wet and incredibly moist, over and over and over.

Curving her arm slowly behind the couch, Francesca withdrew one small flat box, then another, and finally one more. She looked at each carefully, touching her fingers lightly to every photograph. There he was in his ponytail and Hawaiian shirt, the latest arrival—how sharp, how warm his profile—and there, two years earlier, in a loosened tuxedo collar—so formal yet so casual—and there, on the oldest, most handled-with-care box of them all, Jeff held the light in his hands, his glowing, firm, gentle hands.

She was ready for him to come. Instinctively she knew he would prefer to arrive in the old, first way, the *Starman* way as opposed to the *Fisher King* way or the *Fabulous Baker Boys* way, the way they met that afternoon six years ago at Sam's Flick Picks. She drew him out in that style, sliding him carefully out of the tight cardboard sleeve, easing him slowly into the dark but inviting maw of the VCR. With her left hand, she stroked PLAY before pressing it fully. With her right, she stroked her now dampening triangle before pressing fully—no, no, not her triangle! It was Jeff's triangle, not hers, not Robert's—it was Jeff Bridges' and Jeff Bridges' alone, present and past and future and present again.

◀ This child did not survive the first taping of PBS's *Barney & Friends* (1992).

Some of Prince's ▶ designs for the symbol that, in its final form, replaced his name in 1993.

PAISLEY PARK STUDIOS

some logo ideas 4 me 2 consider

:)

PRINCE

4U

make guitar this shape ↰

During the development phase of the politically conservative Fox News Channel, the following shows were the linchpins of the network's schedule: *The Non-Gay Entertainment Report*, *Bruce Willis Reads Onerous Environmental Regulations Aloud*, and, for children, *Muppet Fetuses*.

ANGELL/CASEY/LEE PRODUCTIONS

To: Warren Littlefield, NBC
From: David Angell, Exec. Producer, "Frasier Crane"
Date: 2/5/92

Warren—

It was great seeing you at lunch the other day. As per our conversation, I've attached our pilot script for the "Cheers" spinoff, "Frasier Crane." Essentially, it's the same character from the original show. To avoid the obvious question (why isn't he hanging out with his pals from "Cheers?"), we've decided to take the show out of Boston—we're going with Seattle, since someone on our staff went there once and says it's nice.

As you've no doubt heard, negotiations with Bebe Neuwirth went nowhere, so there won't be any Lilith Crane on the show. We considered asking Shelley Long to play Diane Chambers, but then we decided we'd sooner put cast-iron skewers through our eyes. And besides, we've come up with a solution we think is dynamite: We're going to acknowledge what everyone has known all along and have Frasier come out of the closet. By the time we join him in the pilot, he's left Lilith and heterosexuality and moved back to Seattle. He gets a job hosting a therapy talk-radio show, and his salt-of-the-earth ex-cop father has moved in with him—imagine the good-cop/Village-People-cop fireworks there! But the character who will be the real break-out star is Frasier's lover—an endearingly fussy, prissy aesthete named Niles, who, like Frasier, also happens to be a psychiatrist. The two dandies swap bitchy wisecracks about about opera, French Romantic literature and whether pinot grigio is gauche. (We're considering giving them a Jack Russell terrier. Too cliché?)

We've got loads of great plots in the works for the first season—Frasier and Niles try to collaborate on a self-help book; Frasier has a midlife crisis after flirting with a hunky young store clerk; Frasier is coerced into taking part in a bachelor auction. This one's going to be a smash.

Best,

David

P.S. Could you please ask John Ratzenberger to stop calling me? Nobody wants to see a show about Cliff. Nobody.

David Angell's original vision for *Frasier* (1993), with Warren Littlefield's response. In a similar development deal four years later, NBC changed Greg, Will's hairstylist lover, into Grace, a straight woman with big hair.

NBC From the Desk of Warren Littlefield

2/10/92

Hey David—

Thanks for the script; looks terrific. One small tweak: don't make 'em gay. (Two words: "Love, Sidney.") But the Niles character is great, so keep him—he'll be Frasier's brother. And don't worry, you won't have to rewrite a thing. Just have your assistant switch the bedroom scenes to the living room, and take out some of the close hugging. Add a hot British housekeeper (female), and you've got it made.

See you at the Emmys—

W.

While adapting Winston Groom's novel *Forrest Gump* for the screen, Paramount Pictures used the working title *American Retard*.

got a milk fetish?

Sure, my nipples are cold. But milk is packed with vitamins and nutrients that active bodies need, and calcium to keep bones strong. Plus, it's psychologically necessary for my sexual gratification.

©1994 Milk Advisory Board "Milk Fetishism" is a registered trademark of the Milk Advisory Board.

SOME QUICK IDEAS FOR THE MILK CAMPAIGN —

WHAT ABOUT:
"GOT THE TASTE OF MILK IN YOUR MOUTH FOR NO REASON? SEE A DOCTOR ABOUT THAT."

ALTERNATIVE:
"GOT SOME MILK FOR LEONARD MALTIN?"

ANOTHER POSS.:
"GOT MILK IN YOUR HAT? YOU DO?. THAT'S REALLY WEIRD. WHO WOULD PUT MILK IN YOUR HAT?"

THIS ONE COULD BE REALLY GREAT — STAR POWER ALWAYS A +:
"SAT IN A BUCKET OF MILK?" (SHOWS A CELEBRITY w/SEAT OF PANTS WHITE & DRENCHED) yes!

After its 1993 fetish campaign disturbed focus groups in the midwest, the Dairy Council took another hit when every celebrity except Robert Urich balked at the idea of sitting in buckets of milk. The council settled for dampening upper lips with Elmer's Glue.

Instead of catering, the group job for the Miami cast of MTV's *The Real World* was supposed to be curating an exhibit on the Crimean War.

Jack Canfield's ▶ grandmother's special cold remedy did not move books the way he hoped.

Butternut Squash Soup
with Green Chili Coriander Chutney for the Soul

Edited by Jack Canfield and Mark Victor Hansen

101 Stories to Open the Wallet and Rekindle Book Sales

THE NOTORIOUS B.I.G.

Liberal Media Bias is Pervasive

PARENTAL ADVISORY EXPLICIT LYRICS

MINIMUM WAGE HIKE

Early gangsta rap was condemned by Senator Joseph Lieberman and other Democrats for reasons other than sex and violence.

Initially Comedy Central had four shows starring Ben Stein: *Turn Ben Stein On*, *Remove Ben Stein's Pants*, *Lick Ben Stein's Penis*, and *Win Ben Stein's Money*.

Liberal Media Bias is Pervasive

1. All Taxpayers Deserve a Tax Cut, Except West Coast Niggaz
2. For My Money, "Mad About You" Is the Best Show on Television
3. Making Your Own Smoothies Is Surprisingly Easy
4. The Ongoing Media Neglect of International Affairs *(feat. Lil' Kim)*
5. Raise My Interest Rates and I'll Cut Ya, Nigga *(feat. Alan Greenspan and Mase)*
6. Mo' Money, Mo' Socio-Economic Divide
7. Sorry, I Didn't Get the Memo, Can You Resend It?
8. The Frustrating Thing about the Health Care Reform Debate *(feat. Charlie Rose)*
9. The CBS Leftwing News with Damn Rather
10. I'm Starting to Have Some Doubts About Susan Sontag
11. My Ghetto Instinct Tells Me Vince Foster Didn't Pop No Cap in His Own Ass
12. Frank Gehry Is Overrated *(feat. Philip Johnson)*
13. Certain People in My Neighborhood Are Loud

6 18012 80002 0

Nintendo 63 came with genital feedback wires, a feature later discontinued due to a sharp rise in truancy.

Tickle Me Elmo appeared after the media reported various misuses of his predecessor, Gently Massage Me Elmo.

A transcript from the first pitch meeting for *Jurassic Park* (1993). Producer Gerald Miller went on to write the most frequently downloaded fan fiction on WillandHollyFinallyDoIt.com.

UNIVERSAL FILMS
AMBLIN ENTERTAINMENT PRODUCTIONS

Minutes from **4/20/91** meeting, 1:30 PM
In attendance:
• **Gerald Miller**, producer
• **Steven Spielberg**
• **Michael Crichton**

Transcript:

GERALD: Steven, Michael, glad we could get together.

STEVEN: Yeah. So. Michael wrote this incredible book about a kind of dinosaur zoo gone haywire. It's sort of *King Kong* meets *Land of the Lost*. By cloning dinosaurs' DNA, a grandfatherly scientist—

GERALD: Yes! I'm with you 200%! I'm already thinking casting. If we can get Harrison Ford to play the father—Steven, he owes you big time for Indiana Jones, you could get him to sign on, right?

MICHAEL: But there's no father in the book. There's a grandfather, but—

GERALD: No, no. You're thinking of Uncle Jack. We'll get to him later—first things first: we could get Macauley Culkin to play Chaka! Will and Holly are a little tougher…Sleestak, though—I bet Bill Laimbeer would jump at the chance to don the ol' green scales again!

STEVEN: Listen, Gerald, I think you're missing the point. Our movie is about a genetic research apocalypse, with state-of-the-art special effects—you won't believe the dinosaurs my people have been working on—

GERALD: Good, good, 'cause that claymation shit they had won't fly these days. So do you think you can get Harrison to sign on for the dad?

MICHAEL: I don't think this is gonna work out. The novel is *Jurassic Park*. We don't want to do *Land of the Lost*. They're two completely different—

GERALD: I'll get hold of the Kroffts and see if anyone has bought the movie rights.

STEVEN: I'm sorry. I just don't think you're right for this project.

GERALD: No worries, I'll take it from here…So you guys got anything else for me?

—END—

Buena Vista Social Club

These cels are part of the prospectus for the Independent Film Cartoon network (IFC), which planned to make indie movies like *Breaking the Waves* into animated series. Cable providers rejected the proposal, so the IFC chose simply to show the movies for which they had already bought the rights.

lair Witch Project

The Sweet Hereafter

t script of *Pulp Fiction* (1994), s briefcase contained six in various colors, overhead ncies with an accompanying index cards, a faxed travel esterday's sports page, the nt Jeffery Deaver paperback, *Newsweek,* and gum.

CLOSETED
Men's Health

How to Please Your Woman in Bed

(Even Though You Don't Find Women Sexually Attractive)

Lycra vs. Spandex

What's Best for the Unit

U.S. Men's Gymnasts:

Who's Hot for the Gold?

Tips for a Thorough Prostate Self-Exam

$5.95US $6.95CAN

0 72440 10093 0

◀ Latently homosexual men did not buy this magazine when it appeared in 1995 on newsstands in public places.

An early sketch for the ▶ cover of *Harry Potter and the Sorcerer's Stone* (1998), the American edition. Each country had its own marketing tie-in: England's cover featured the Virgin logo, and Australia's had a can of Foster's.

PlayStation

"Oprah's Beer ▶
Club"—her 1994
campaign to help
wives of alcoholic
husbands kick
back and enjoy
themselves—
failed miserably.
She recouped
her losses by
promoting books
about wives
of alcoholic
husbands.

▌ Thanks to the proceeds from
OK Computer (1997), the
members of Radiohead were
able to make their secret
fantasies come true in this
beta release of *Kid A*.
The album's first track,
"Freak U Up," begins, "Girl,
you bring out/The karma
police in me/Groovin' to the
music/Jammin' with me."

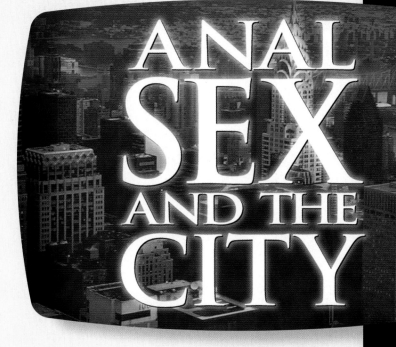

HBO eventually ▶ decided to make anal sex a recurring theme instead of the basis for the entire show.

p. 140

INT. CAL'S PARLOUR SUITE

Water swirls in from the private promenade deck. Rose's paintings are submerged. The Picasso tranforms under the water's surface. Degas' colors run. Monet's water lilies come to life. The Mona Lisa floats by in the foreground. The bookshelves on the walls creak and fall into the water, carrying with them Leonardo da Vinci's notebooks; placed in the notebooks as a bookmark, a Honus Wagner baseball card falls out and is quickly lost under the water. The ship lurches and the cabin tilts sharply, bringing an original Ford Model T crashing through the wall--right through Cezanne's Apples and Pears, alas. The car's grille smashes into a precious Ming vase, which shatters. Unfortunately, that Ming vase was holding up a shelf of Egyptian artifacts, rescued from the tomb of King Tutankhamen; they fall into the water and quickly dissolve to mud. The car's door falls open, and the Venus de Milo--which had been perched in the driver's seat--tumbles out and breaks in two as it hits the desk. This, in turn, causes the desk to tip into the brine, bearing with it the original draft of the Gettysburg Address. The camera follow the Address as it falls into the water and sinks, coming to rest atop the Dead Sea Scrolls, the Constitution and the Book of Kells.

[NOTE: This sequence must be filmed with the actual objects, or I walk. --JC]

◀ At $200 million, the *Titanic* (1997) budget was big but not big enough for James Cameron's artistic vision. In addition to cutting back the scene shown here, Cameron also had to relinquish plans to drown real people, travel back in time, and have a well-written screenplay.

When NBA ▶ executives first tried to diversify their market, they tested professional children's basketball, but labor laws got in the way. Next came dogs (the K9BA, shown here), then Friends of NBA Players, then Friends of Friends, then Men in Bras, and, finally, the WNBA.

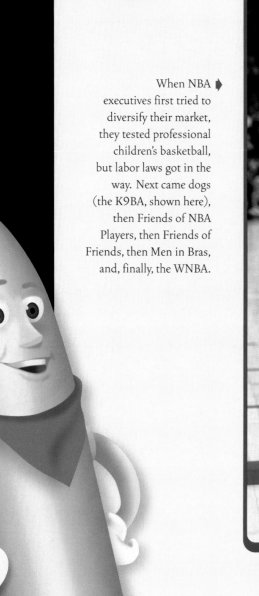

◀ Pixar released *Sex Toy Story*, with its cutting-edge computer animation, to the pornographic video market in 1994. In addition to Woody the Dildo (shown here), the feature starred Kinky Dog, Buzz the Vibrator, and Tyrannosaurus Cock.

Trey Parker and Matt Stone first imagined *South Park* (1997) with a girls-only cast. In the pilot, members of the group discover one by one that blood is being periodically secreted by their uteri.

From George Lucas's early sketches for *The Phantom Menace* (1999): Jar Jar Binks, to be played by Robert Urich.

The Hearst ▶
Corporation
jumped at the
idea of a magazine
headed by a
fantastically
successful talk-show
host with legions
of worshipful
fans. This was
their first attempt.

J

THE JERRY MAGAZINE

TOO HOT FOR
NEWSSTANDS!

YOU HO, GIRL!

Be the best skank
your ass can be

JUNE, 2000 $2.95

01>
0 00000 0

BITCH THINK SHE ALL THAT
But shhh!
She's a **man**

◀ Jennifer Lopez at the pre-party
for the 2000 Grammy Awards
before she changed into a more
tasteful outfit.

In addition to their
"lollipop" colors, the
first iMacs had chewy
chocolate centers.

CONTENTS
Premiere Issue

"JER-RY! JER-RY! JER-RY JER-RY!"

Final Thoughts

Take care of yourself and each other, but if it doesn't work out, call 1-800-SPRINGER.

159 DUTCH TEAT: Imported pacifiers and other must-haves.

100 FEELING SAUCY: The meal he deserves.

200 STAMP OF APPROVAL: That sixth kid sure paid off.

For the final tribal council on the first *Survivor* (2000), Sue had prepared a much more detailed speech.

Kelly, you remember when Jeff said "what goes around comes around?" Probably not, because I wouldn't expect a developmentally disabled individual like you to have a good memory. But this is when it comes around. If you should win tonight, I'll shake your hand and go on from here, but if I was ever to pass you along in life again, and you were dying of thirst,

I would not give you any water. Instead I would gouge out your eyes with a spoon and drive a railroad spike through each of your kneecaps. And then I would jump up and down on your face, light a cigarette and stick it in your eye, and look through your pockets for change. Then I

would take a piece of extra-coarse sandpaper and rub it back and forth over your wounds, and after that I would infect you with the flesh-eating strep virus and then violate you with a fork, and then I would spit on you. But I would spit on you right in the middle of your back, where you can't reach, so that you couldn't possibly get any moisture from my spit, because if you recall, you were dying of thirst, and I wouldn't want to do anything to ruin that. And then I would photograph you so that years from now I could show my grandchildren what happens to back-stabbing degenerates like you. And then I would shake your hand and go on from there.

I plead to the jury tonight to think a little bit about the island that we have been on. This island is pretty much full of only two things: snakes and rats. And Richard is sly, and regularly sheds his skin, like a snake, while Kelly is cowardly, has a pointed nose, likes to root around in garbage, and can gnaw through wood, like a rat. And I say it's time for the snake to eat the rat, first sinking its venomous fangs deep into the rat's flesh, and paralyzing it, unless we're talking about a python or anaconda, in which case it would first suffocate the rat by crushing it within its coils, then swallowing it whole, moving it through its digestive tract

by peristalsis, dissolving it with gastric acid, breaking it down with enzymes, absorbing its nutrients, and finally excreting it like the piece of shit Kelly is.

To recap: Kelly, bad.

Thank you.

◀ Britney Spears wore this shirt for sound check but never in concert because she didn't like the font.

Because of contractual difficulties, *Being John Malkovich* (1999) could not be titled *Being John Ritter*.

In their early mall ▶ appearances, the Backstreet Boys made young girls shriek and run away.

backstreet boys

Many organizations and individuals have kindly lent their property and knowledge to this project. We are especially indebted to:

The Antique Thong Enthusiasts of America

The Estates of Orson Welles, Alfred Hitchcock, Frank Zappa, Tupac Shakur and Larry "Midget" Flanagan

Dr. Robert Oppenheimer and the Farrah Fawcett Project

The Brandon Tartikoff Training School

Jimmy & Rosalynn Carter

The Anti Pack-Rat-Defamation League

Sir Andrew Lloyd Webber's Personal Time Capsule

Friends of ZZ Top

The *Three's Company* Collection of Rare Books and Manuscripts

Hunter S. Thompson's Mom

Lucasfilm Ltd.

Institute for the Study of Irish Iconography, Leprechaun Division

The Boston Women's Health Book Collective

The *Diff'rent Strokes* Reenactment Society, Philadelphia Squad No. 813

Sotheby's

J.D. Salinger's Box of Secret Stuff

The National Museum of Suction-Cupped Decorations for the American Automobile

Mr. & Mrs. Rodney P. Dangerfield

The Keepers of Obscure, Forgotten, but Not Necessarily Terrible Television Pilots

The Linda Lovelace Library and Resource Center

Mary Tyler Moore's Recycling Pile

The Christian Broadcasting Network

The Basements of Neil Simon, Brooke Shields, Prince, and Julia Louis-Dreyfus

Roman Polanski's Little Brother

The *Dirty Dancing* Cabinet of Wonders

M. Night Shyamalan

The PONG People of Sacramento

Yoko Ono

The Society for the Preservation of Meaty Legos

The Robert Urich Collection

■

NOTES ON THE TYPE

Rough Draft was typeset using the following type families:
the Gill Sans family from Adobe, the Vendetta family from
Emigre fonts, the Rhode family from the Font Bureau
and the Partridge family of San Pueblo, California.
Originally, the book was going to be set all in Helvetica,
only really really big, with a cool 3-D effect and sort
of a rainbow drop shadow thing, but some people
just have *no* imagination, you know?

■